Piracy, Turtles and
Flying Foxes

Sumatra, 1686

WILLIAM DAMPIER

Piracy, Turtles and Flying Foxes

GREAT
JOURNEYS

TED SMART

PENGUIN BOOKS

Published by the Penguin Group
Penguin Books Ltd, 80 Strand, London WC2R ORL, England
Penguin Group (USA) Inc., 375 Hudson Street, New York, New York 10014, USA
Penguin Group (Canada), 90 Eglinton Avenue East, Suite 700, Toronto, Ontario, Canada M4P 2Y3
(a division of Pearson Penguin Canada Inc.)
Penguin Ireland, 25 St Stephen's Green, Dublin 2, Ireland (a division of Penguin Books Ltd)
Penguin Group (Australia), 250 Camberwell Road, Camberwell, Victoria 3124, Australia
(a division of Pearson Australia Group Pty Ltd)
Penguin Books India Pvt Ltd, 11 Community Centre, Panchsheel Park, New Delhi – 110 017, India
Penguin Group (NZ), 67 Apollo Drive, Rosedale, North Shore 0632, New Zealand
(a division of Pearson New Zealand Ltd)
Penguin Books (South Africa) (Pty) Ltd, 24 Sturdee Avenue, Rosebank, Johannesburg 2196, South Africa

Penguin Books Ltd, Registered Offices: 80 Strand, London WC2R ORL, England

www.penguin.com

A New Voyage Round the World first published 1697
This extract published in Penguin Books 2007
3

All rights reserved

Inside-cover maps by Jeff Edwards

Typeset by Rowland Phototypesetting Ltd, Bury St Edmunds, Suffolk
Printed in England by Clays Ltd, St Ives plc

ISBN: 978-0-141-02541-4

This edition produced for The Book People Ltd,
Hall Wood Avenue, Haydock, St. Helens, WA11 9UL

Contents

William Dampier (1651–1715) had a long and un-
believably chaotic career, managing more by accident
than design to sail around the world three times and
participate in a wilderness of almost uniformly unsuc-
cessful piratical and semi-piratical ventures. At a low
point in his career, broke and back in London, he wrote
A New Voyage Round the World, the first great travel
book in English. In it he recounts his adventures, first
in the Caribbean and Spain's Pacific empire, then
across Southeast Asia, Australia (of which he gives the
first account in English) and home via the Cape of
Good Hope. The book had an immense impact on a
generation of writers, including Defoe, Swift and Pope
and remains a marvellously vivid picture of people,
places, animals and plants – as well as being an unfor-
gettable account of the life of a failed pirate.

In later years Dampier went on first to lead a wholly
mishandled expedition to Australia and then – at last
– to become very rich piloting a raid on a Spanish
treasure-ship.

These extracts highlight several of his most memor-
able exploits.

Preface

Before the Reader proceeds any further in the perusal of this Work, I must bespeak a little of his Patience here to take along with him this short account of it. It is composed of a Mixed Relation of Places and Actions, in the same order of time in which they occurred, for which end I kept a Journal of every Day's Observations.

In the Description of Places, their Product, &c., I have endeavoured to give what satisfaction I could to my Countrymen, though possibly describing several things that may have been much better accounted for by others. I have chosen to be more particular than might be needful, with respect to the intelligent Reader, rather than to omit what I thought might tend to the Information of Persons no less sensible and inquisitive, though not so Learned or Experienced. For this reason, my chief Care has been to be as particular as was consistent with my intended brevity, in setting down such Observables as I met with. Nor have I given myself any great Trouble, since my Return, to compare my Discoveries with those of others. Rather, because, should it so happen that I have described some places or things which others have done before me, yet in different Accounts, even of the same things, it can hardly be but there will be some new Light afforded by each of them. But after all, considering that the main of this Voyage has its Scene laid in long Tracts of the Remoter Parts, both of the East and West Indies, some of which very seldom visited by Englishmen, and others as rarely by any Europeans, I may without vanity encourage the Reader to expect many things wholly new to him, and many others more fully described than he may have seen elsewhere. For not only this Voyage, though itself of many years' continuance, but also several former long and distant Voyages have qualified me for this.

As for the Actions of the Company among whom I made the greatest part of this Voyage, a Thread of which I have carried on through it, it is not to divert the Reader with them that I mention them, much less that I take any pleasure in relating them. But I do this for method's sake, and for the Reader's satisfaction, who could not so well acquiesce in my Description of Places, &c. without knowing the particular Traverses I made among them, nor in these, without an Account of the Concomitant Circumstances. Besides, I could not prejudice the Truth and Sincerity of my Relation, though by Omissions only. And as for the Traverses themselves, they make for the Reader's advantage, how little soever for mine, since thereby I have been the better enabled to gratify his Curiosity; as one who rambles about a Country can give usually a better account of it, than a Carrier who jogs on to his Inn, without ever going out of his Road.

*

As to my Style, it cannot be expected that a Seaman should affect Politeness. For were I able to do it, yet I think I should be little solicitous about it in a work of this Nature. I have frequently indeed divested myself of Sea-Phrases to gratify the Land Reader, for which the Seamen will hardly forgive me. And yet, possibly, I shall not seem complaisant enough to the other, because I still retain the use of so many Sea-terms. I confess I have not been at all scrupulous in this matter, either as to the one or the other of these. For I am persuaded that if what I say is intelligible, it does not matter greatly in what words it is expressed.

For the same Reason I have not been curious as to the spelling of the Names of Places, Plants, Fruits, Animals, &c. which in any of these remoter parts are given at the pleasure of Travellers, and vary according to their different Humours. Neither have I confined myself to such Names as are given by learned Authors, or so much as enquired after many of them. I write for my Countrymen, and have therefore, for the most part, used such Names as are familiar to our English Seamen, and those of our Colonies abroad, yet without neglecting others that occurred. As it might suffice me to have given such Names and Descriptions as I could, I shall leave to those of more leisure and opportunity the trouble of comparing these with the ones which other Authors have assigned.

I have nothing more to add, but that there are, here and there, some mistakes made, as to expression and the like, which will need a favourable Correction as they occur upon Reading. In other places also I may not have expressed myself so fully as I ought. But any considerable Omission that I shall recollect or be informed of, I shall endeavour to make up in those Accounts I have yet to publish. And for any Faults, I leave the Reader to the joint use of his Judgement and Candour.

Introduction

I first set out of England on this Voyage at the beginning of the year 1679, in the *Loyal Merchant* of London, bound for Jamaica, Captain Knapman Commander. I went a Passenger, designing when I came there to go from there to the Bay of Campeachy in the Gulf of Mexico to cut Logwood, where in a former Voyage I had spent about three years in that employ. And so I was well acquainted with the place and the work.

We sailed with a prosperous Gale without any impediment or remarkable Passage in our Voyage, except that when we came in Sight of the Island Hispaniola, and were coasting along on the South-side of it, by the little Isles of Vacca, or Ash, I observed Captain Knapman was more vigilant than ordinary, keeping at a good distance offshore, for fear of coming too near those small low Islands. He did this once, in a Voyage from England, about the Year 1673, losing his Ship there by the Carelessness of his Mates. But we succeeded better, and arrived safe at Port Royal in Jamaica some time in April 1679 and went immediately ashore.

I had brought some Goods with me from England, which I intended to sell here, and stock myself with Rum and Sugar, Saws, Axes, Hats, Stockings, Shoes and such other Commodities, as I knew would sell among the

Campeachy Logwood-cutters. Accordingly I sold my English cargo at Port Royal, but upon some maturer Considerations of my intended Voyage to Campeachy, I changed my Thoughts of that design, and continued at Jamaica all that Year, in Expectation of some other Business.

I shall not trouble the Reader with my Observations at that Isle, so well known to Englishmen, nor with the Particulars of my own Affairs during my Stay there. But in short, having there made a Purchase of a small Estate in Dorsetshire, near my Native Country of Somerset, from one whose Title to it I was well assured of, I was just embarking myself for England, about Christmas 1679, when one Mr Hobby invited me to go first a short Trading Voyage to the Country of the Moskitos, of whom I shall speak in my first Chapter. I was willing to get up some Money before my return, having laid out what I had at Jamaica. So I sent the Writing of my new Purchase along with the same Friends whom I should have accompanied to England, and went on board with Mr Hobby.

Soon after our setting out we came to an anchor again in Negril Bay, at the West-end of Jamaica, but finding there Captains Coxon, Sawkins, Sharp, and other Privateers, Mr Hobby's Men all left him to go with them, upon an Expedition they had contrived, leaving not one with him beside myself; and being thus left alone, after three or four Days' stay with Mr Hobby, I was the more easily persuaded to go with them too.

*

It was shortly after Christmas 1679 when we set out. The first Expedition was to Portobello, which being accomplished, it was resolved to march by Land over the Isthmus of Darien, upon some new Adventures in the South Seas. Accordingly on the 5th of April 1680, we went ashore on the Isthmus, near Golden Island, one of the Samballoes, to the Number of between three and four hundred Men, carrying with us such Provisions as were necessary, and Toys with which to gratify the Wild Indians, through whose Country we were to pass. In about nine Days' march we arrived at Santa Maria and took it, and after a Stay there of about three Days, we went on to the South Sea Coast, and there embarked ourselves in such Canoes and Periagos as our Indian Friends furnished us with. We were in Sight of Panama by the 23rd of April, and having in vain attempted Puebla Nova, before which Sawkins, then Commander-in-chief, and others, were killed, we made a Stay at the neighbouring Isles of Quibo.

Here we resolved to change our Course, and stand away to the Southward for the Coast of Peru. Accordingly we left the Isles of Quibo the 6th of June, and spent the rest of the Year on that Southern Course. For touching at the Isles of Gorgonia and Plata, we came to Ylo, a small Town on the Coast of Peru, and took it. This was in October, and in November we went from there to Coquimbo on the same Coast, and about Christmas had got as far as the Isle of John Fernando, which was the farthest of our Course to the Southward.

*

After Christmas we went back again to the Northward, having a design upon Arica, a strong Town advantageously situated in the hollow of the Elbow, or bending, of the Peruvian Coast. But being repulsed there with great Loss, we continued our Course Northward, till by the middle of April we had come in sight of the Isle of Plata, a little to the Southward of the Equinoctial Line.

I have related this part of my Voyage thus summarily and concisely because the World has Accounts of it already, in the relations that Mr Ringrose and others have given of Captain Sharp's Expedition, who was made chief Commander upon Sawkins' being killed; also because, in the prosecution of this Voyage, I shall come to speak of these parts again, upon occasion of my going the second time into the South Seas. And I shall there describe at large the Places both of North and South America, as they occurred to me. And for this Reason, so that I might avoid needless Repetitions, and hasten to such particulars as the Public has hitherto had no account of, I have chosen to comprise the Relation of my Voyage hitherto in this short Compass, and place it as an Introduction before the rest, so that the Reader may better perceive where I mean to begin to be particular. For there I have placed the Title of my first Chapter.

All therefore that I have to add to the Introduction is this: that while we lay at the Isle of John Fernando, Captain Sharp was, by general Consent, displaced from

being Commander, the Company being not satisfied
either with his Courage or Behaviour. In his stead,
Captain Watling was advanced, but he being killed
shortly after Arica, we were without a Commander
during all the rest of our Return towards Plata. Now
Watling being killed, a great Number of the meaner
sort began to be as earnest for choosing Captain Sharp
again into the Vacancy, as before they had been as
forward as any to turn him out. And on the other side,
the abler and more experienced Men, being altogether
dissatisfied with Sharp's former Conduct, would by no
means consent to have him chosen. In short, by the
time we had come in Sight of the Island Plata, the
difference between the contending Parties had grown
so high, that they resolved to part Companies, having
first made an Agreement that whichever Party should
upon Polling appear to have the Majority, they should
keep the Ship. And the others should content themselves with the Launch and Canoes, and return back
over the Isthmus, or go to seek their Fortune in other
ways, as they would.

Accordingly we put it to the Vote, and upon dividing,
Captain Sharp's Party carried it. I, who had never been
pleased with his Management (though I had hitherto
kept my Mind to myself) now declared myself on the
side of those that were outvoted, and according to our
Agreement, we took our Shares of such Necessaries as
were fit to carry over Land with us (for that was our
Resolution), and so prepared for our Departure.

From the South Seas Overland to the Caribbean

April the 17th 1681, about Ten o'clock in the Morning, being 12 Leagues NW from the Island Plata, we left Captain Sharp and those who were willing to go with him in the Ship, and embarked into our Launch and Canoes, designing for the River of Santa Maria, in the Gulf of St Michael, which is about 200 Leagues from the Isle of Plata. We were in Number 44 white Men who bore Arms; a Spanish Indian, who bore Arms also; and two Moskito Indians, who always bear Arms amongst the Privateers, and are much valued by them for striking Fish, Turtle (or Tortoise), and Manatee (or Sea-Cow); and five Slaves taken in the South Seas, who fell to our share.

The Craft which carried us was a Launch (or Long-boat), one Canoe, and another Canoe, which had been sawn asunder in the Middle, in order to make Bumkins, or Vessels for carrying Water, if we had not separated from our Ship. This we joined together again and made it tight, providing Sails to help us along. And for three Days before we parted, we sifted as much Flour as we could well carry, and rubbed up 20 or 30 pounds of Chocolate, with Sugar to sweeten it. These things and a Kettle, the Slaves carried on their Backs after we landed. And because there were some who designed to go with us that we knew were not well able to march, we gave out that if any Man faltered in the Journey over Land, he must expect to be shot to Death. For we knew that the Spaniards would soon be after us, and one Man falling into their Hands might be the ruin of us all, by giving an account of our Strength and Condition. Yet this would not deter 'em from going with us. We had but little wind when we parted from the Ship, but before 12 o'clock, the Sea-breeze came in strong, which was likely to founder us before we got in with the shore. For our security therefore, we cut up an old dry Hide that we had brought with us, and barricaded the Launch all round with it to keep the Water out. About 10 o'clock at Night we got in about 7 Leagues to Windward of Cape Passao under the Line, and then it proved calm. And we lay and drove all Night, being fatigued the preceding Day. The 18th Day we had little Wind till the Afternoon; and then we made sail, standing along the shore to the Northward, having the Wind at S.S.W. and fair Weather.

At 7 o'clock we came abreast of Cape Passao, and found a small Bark at an Anchor in a small Bay to Leeward of the Cape, which we took, our own Boats being too small to transport us. We took her just under the Equinoctial Line. She was not only a help to us, but in taking her, we were safe from being descried. We did not design to meddle with anyone when we parted with our Consorts, nor to see anyone if we could have helped it. The Bark came from Galleo, laden with Timber, and was bound for Guayaquil.

*

The 19th Day in the Morning we came to an Anchor about 12 Leagues to the Southward of Cape St Francisco, to put our new Bark into a better trim. In 3 or 4 Hours' time we finished our Business and came to sail again, and steered along the Coast with the Wind at S.S.W., intending to touch at Gorgonia.

Being to the Northward of Cape St Francisco we met with very wet Weather. But the Wind continuing, we arrived at Gorgonia the 24th Day in the Morning, before it was light. We were afraid to approach it in the Daytime, for fear the Spaniards should lie there for us, it being the place where we careened lately, and there they might be expecting us.

When we came ashore we found the Spaniards had been there to seek after us, by a House they had built, which would entertain 100 Men, and by a great Cross before the Doors. This was token enough that the Spaniards expected us this Day again. Therefore we examined our Prisoners if they knew anything of it, who confessed they had heard of a Periago (or large Canoe), that rowed with 14 Oars, which was kept in a River on the Main, and once in 2 or three Days came over to Gorgonia purposely to see for us. And having discovered us, she was to make all speed to Panama with the News, where they had three Ships ready to send after us.

We lay here all Day, and scrubbed our new Bark so that, if ever we should be chased, we might better escape. We filled our Water, and in the Evening went from there, having the Wind at S.W., a brisk gale.

The 25th Day we had much Wind and Rain, and we lost the Canoe that had been cut and joined together. We would have kept all our Canoes to carry us up the River, the Bark not being so convenient.

The 27th Day we went from there with a moderate gale of Wind at S.W. In the Afternoon, we had excessive Showers of Rain.

The 28th Day was very wet all Morning. Between 10 and 11 it cleared up, and we saw two great Ships about a League and a half to the Westward of us, we being then two Leagues from the shore, and about 10 Leagues to the Southward of Point Garrachina. These Ships had been cruising between Gorgonia and the Gulf 6 Months, but whether our Prisoners knew it, I cannot tell.

We presently furled our Sails, and rowed in close under the shore, knowing that they were Cruisers. For if they had been bound to Panama, this Wind would have carried them here. And no Ships bound from Panama come on this side of the Bay, but keep the North-side of the Bay till as far as the Keys of Quibo to the Westward. And then, if they are bound to the South-ward, they stand over and may fetch Galleo, or between there and Cape St Francisco.

*

The Glare did not continue long before it rained again, and kept us from the sight of each other. But if they had seen and chased us, we were resolved to run our Bark and Canoes ashore, and take ourselves to the Mountains and travel over Land. For we knew that the Indians which lived in these parts never had any Commerce with the Spaniards, so we might have had a chance for our Lives.

The 29th Day, at 9 o'clock in the Morning, we came to an Anchor at Point Garrachina, about 7 Leagues from the Gulf of St Michael, which was the Place where we first came into the South Seas, and the way by which we designed to return. Here we lay all Day, and went ashore and dried our Clothes, cleaned our Guns, dried our Ammunition, and fixed ourselves against our Enemies, if we should be attacked, for we expected to find some Opposition at Landing. We likewise kept a good Lookout all the Day, for fear of those two Ships that we saw the Day before.

The 30th Day in the Morning at 8 o'clock, we came into the Gulf of St Michael's Mouth. For we had put from Point Garrachina in the Evening, designing to reach the Islands in the Gulf before Day, so that we might better work our Escape from our Enemies, if we should find any of them waiting to stop our Passage.

About 9 o'clock we came to an Anchor a Mile off a large Island, which lies 4 Miles from the Mouth of the River. We had other small Islands without us, and might have gone up into the River, having a strong flood tide, but would not adventure farther till we had looked well about us.

We immediately sent a Canoe ashore on the Island, where we saw (what we always feared) a Ship at the Mouth of the River, lying close by the shore, and a large Tent by it, by which we found it would be a hard Task for us to escape them.

When the Canoe came aboard with this News, some of our Men were a little disheartened. But it was no more than I ever expected.

Our Care was now to get safe over Land, seeing we could not land here according to our desire. Therefore, before the flood tide was spent, we manned our Canoe and rowed again to the Island to see if the Enemy was yet in Motion. When we came ashore we dispersed ourselves all over the Island, to prevent our Enemies from coming any way to view us. And presently, after high Water, we saw a small Canoe coming over from the Ship to the Island that we were on. This made us all get into our Canoes and wait their coming. And we lay close till they came within Pistol-shot of us, and then being ready, we started out and took them. There were in her one white Man and two Indians who, being examined, told us that the Ship which we saw at the River's Mouth had lain there six Months, guarding the River, and waiting for our coming. She had 12 Guns, and 150 Seamen and Soldiers. The Seamen all lay aboard, but the Soldiers lay ashore in their Tents. There were 300 Men at the Mines, who all had small Arms, and would be aboard in two tides' Time. They likewise told us that there were two Ships cruising in the Bay, between this place and Gorgonia. The biggest had 20 Guns and 200 Men, the other 10 Guns and 150 Men. Besides all this they told us that the Indians on this side of the Country were our Enemies, which was the worst News of all. However we presently brought these Prisoners aboard, and got under sail, turning out with the Ebb-tide, for it was not convenient to stay longer there.

We did not long consider what to do, but intended to land that Night or early the next Day. For we did not question that we should either get a good Commerce with the Indians, by such Toys as we had purposely brought with us, or else force our way through their Country, in spite of all their Opposition. And we did not fear what these Spaniards could do against us, in case they should land and come after us. We had a strong Southerly wind, which blew right in, and the Ebb tide being far spent, we could not turn out.

I persuaded them to run into the River Congo, which is a large River, about three Leagues from the Island where we lay. With a Southerly Wind we could have done this, and when we had got as high as the Tide flows, then we might have landed. But all the Arguments I could use were not of force sufficient to convince them that there was a large River so near us.

They were going to land somewhere, but they neither knew how, where, nor when.

When we had rowed and rowed against the Wind all Night, we just got about Cape St Lorenzo in the Morning and sailed about 4 Miles farther to the Westward, running into a small Creek within two Keys, and rowing up to the Head of the Creek, which was about a Mile up, and there we landed May 1st 1681.

We got out all our Provision and Clothes, and then sunk our Vessel.

While we were landing and fixing our Snap-sacks to march, our Moskito Indians struck a plentiful Dish of Fish, which we immediately dressed, and satisfied our Hunger.

Having made Mention of the Moskito Indians, it may not be amiss to conclude this Chapter with a short account of them. They are tall, well made, raw-boned, lusty, strong, and nimble of Foot, long-visaged, lank black Hair, stern of look, hard-favoured, and of a dark Copper-coloured Complexion. They are but a small Nation or Family, and not 100 Men of them in Number, inhabiting the main on the North-side, near Cape Gratia Dios, between Cape Honduras and Nicaragua. They are very ingenious at throwing the Lance, Fizgig, Harpoon, or any manner of Dart, being bred to it from their Infancy. For the Children, imitating their Parents, never go abroad without a Lance in their Hands, which they throw at any Object, till use has made them Masters of the Art. Then they learn to put by a Lance, Arrow, or Dart. The manner is thus: two Boys stand at a small distance and dart a blunt stick at one another, each of them holding a small stick in his right Hand, with which he strikes away what was darted at him. As they grow in years they become more dextrous and courageous, and then they will stand a fair Mark to anyone that will shoot Arrows at them, which they will put by with a very small stick, no bigger than the Rod of a Fowling-piece. And when they are grown to be Men, they will guard themselves from Arrows, though they come very thick at them, provided two do not happen to come at once. They have extra-ordinarily good Eyes, and will descry a Sail at Sea farther, and see anything better than we. Their chiefest Employment in their own Country is to strike Fish, Turtle or Manatee. For this they are esteemed and coveted by all Privateers. For one or two of them in a Ship will maintain 100 Men, so that when we careen our Ships, we choose commonly such Places where there is plenty of Turtle or Manatee for these Moskito Men to strike: and it is very rare to find Privateers destitute of one or more of them, when the Com-mander or most of the Men are English. But they do not love the French, and the Spaniards they hate mortally. When they come among Privateers, they get the use of Guns, and prove very good Marksmen. They behave themselves very boldly in fight, and never seem to flinch nor hang back. For they think that the white Men with whom they are, know better than they do when it is best to fight, and they will never let the disadvantage of their Party be so great as to yield or give back while any of their Party stand. I never perceived any Religion, nor any Ceremonies or superstitious Observations among them, being ready to imitate us in whatsoever they saw us do at any time. Only they seem to fear the Devil, whom they call *Wallesaw*. And they say he often appears to some among them, whom our Men commonly call their Priest, when they desire to speak with him on urgent business. But the rest know nothing of him, nor how he appears, otherwise than what these Priests tell them. Yet they all say they must not anger him, for then he will beat them, and that sometimes he carries away these Priests of theirs. This much I have heard from some of them who speak good English.

They marry but one Wife, with whom they live till Death separates them. At their first coming together, the Man makes a very small Plantation, for there is Land enough, and they may choose whatever spot they please. They delight to settle near the Sea, or by some River, for the sake of striking Fish, their beloved Employment.

Within Land there are other Indians, with whom they are always at War. After the Man has cleared a spot of Land, and has planted it, he seldom minds it afterwards, but leaves the managing of it to his Wife, and he goes out striking. Sometimes he seeks only for Fish, at other times for Turtle, or Manatee, and whatever he gets he brings home to his Wife, and never stirs out to seek for more till it is all eaten. When Hunger begins to bite, he either takes his Canoe and seeks for more Game at Sea, or walks out into the Woods and hunts about for Peccary or Warree, each a sort of wild Hog or Deer, seldom returning empty-handed, nor seeking for any more, so long as any of it lasts. Their Plantations are so small that they cannot subsist with what they produce. For their largest Plantations do not have above 20 or 30 Plantain-Trees, a Bed of Yams and Potatoes, a Bush of Indian Pepper, and a small spot of Pine-apples. This last Fruit is the main thing they delight in, for with these they make a sort of Drink which our Men call Pine-drink, much esteemed by these Moskitos, and to which they invite each other to be merry, providing Fish and Flesh also. Whoever of them makes this Liquor treats his Neighbours, making a little Canoe-full at a time, and so enough to make them all drunk. It is seldom that such Feasts are made without the Party that makes them having some design, either to be revenged for some Injury done him, or to debate of such Differences as have happened between him and his Neighbours, and to examine into the Truth of such Matters. Yet before they are warmed with drink, they never speak one word of their Grievances, and the Women, who commonly know their Husband's Designs, prevent them from doing any injury to each other by hiding their Lances, Harpoons, Bows and Arrows, or any other Weapon that they have.

*

The Moskitos are in general very civil and kind to the English, from whom they receive a great deal of Respect, both when they are aboard their Ships, and also ashore, either in Jamaica, or elsewhere, where they often come with the Seamen. We always humour them, letting them go anywhere they will, and return to their Country in any Vessel bound that way, if they please. They will have the Management of themselves in their striking, and will go in their own little Canoe, which our Men could not go in without danger of oversetting. Nor will they then let any white Man come in their Canoe, but will go striking in it just as they please, all of which we allow them. For should we cross them, though they should see Shoals of Fish, or Turtle, or the like, they will purposely strike their Harpoons and Turtle-irons aside, or so glance them as to kill nothing. They have no form of Government among them, but acknowledge the King of England for their Sovereign. They learn our Language, and take the Governor of Jamaica to be one of the greatest Princes in the World.

While they are among the English they wear good Clothes, and take delight to go neat and tight. But when they return again to their own Country they put by all their Clothes, and go after their own Country fashion, wearing only a small Piece of Linen tied about their Waists, hanging down to their Knees.

Having landed May the 1st, we began our march about 3 o'clock in the Afternoon, directing our Course by our pocket Compasses N. E. After about 2 Miles, we came to the Foot of a Hill where we built small Huts and lay all Night, having excessive Rains till 12 o'clock.

The 2nd Day in the Morning, having fair Weather, we ascended the Hill, and found a small Indian Path, which we followed till we found it ran too much Easterly. Then, doubting it would carry us out of the way, we climbed some of the highest Trees on the Hill, which was not meanly furnished with as large and tall Trees as ever I saw. At length we discovered some Houses in a Valley on the North-side of the Hill, but it being steep, we could not descend on that Side, but followed the small Path which led us down the Hill on the East-side, where we presently found several other Indian Houses. The first that we came to at the Foot of the Hill had only some Women at home, who could not speak Spanish, but gave each of us a good Calabash or Shell-full of Corn-drink. The other Houses had some Men at home, but none that spoke Spanish. Yet we made a shift to buy such Food as their Houses or Plantations afforded, which we dressed and ate all together, having all sorts of our Provision in common, because no-one should live better than the others, or pay dearer for anything than it was worth. This Day we had marched 6 Miles.

In the Evening the Husbands of these Women came home, and told us in broken Spanish that they had been on board the Guard-Ship that we had fled from two Days before, and that we were now no more than 3 Miles from the Mouth of the River Congo, and that they could go from there aboard the Guard-Ship in half a tide's Time.

This Evening we supped plentifully on Fowls, and Peccary, a sort of wild Hog which we bought off the Indians. Yams, Potatoes and Plantains served us for Bread, of which we had sufficient. After Supper we agreed with one of these Indians to Guide us a Day's march into the Country, towards the North-side. He was to have for his Pains a Hatchet, and his bargain was to bring us to a certain Indian's Habitation, who could speak Spanish, from whom we were in hopes to be better satisfied of our Journey.

The 3rd Day, having fair Weather, we began to stir early, and set out between 6 and 7 o'clock, marching through several old ruined Plantations. This Morning, one of our Men being tired gave us the slip. By 12 o'clock we had gone 8 Miles, and arrived at the Indian's House, who lived on the Bank of the River Congo, and spoke very good Spanish. To him we declared the Reason of this Visit.

At first he seemed to be very dubious of entertaining any Discourse with us, and gave impertinent Answers to the Questions that we demanded of him. He told us he knew no way to the North-side of the Country, but could carry us to Cheapo or Santa Maria, which we knew to be Spanish Garrisons, one lying to the Eastward of us, the other to the Westward, either of them at least 20 Miles out of our way. We could get no other answer from him, and all his Discourse was in such an angry Tone as plainly declared he was not our Friend. However, we were forced to make a Virtue of Necessity, and humour him, for it was neither time nor place to be angry with the Indians, with all our lives lying in their Hands.

We were now at a great Loss, not knowing what Course to take, for we tempted him with Beads, Money, Hatchets, Machetes and long Knives. But nothing would work on him till one of our Men took a Sky-coloured Petticoat out of his Bag and put it on his Wife. She was so much pleased with the Present, that she immediately began to chatter to her Husband, and soon brought him into a better Humour. He was then able to tell us that he knew the way to the North-side, and would have gone with us, only he had cut his Foot two Days before, which made him incapable of serving us himself. But he would take Care that we should not want for a Guide. Therefore he hired the same Indian who had brought us here, to conduct us two Days' march further for another Hatchet. The old Man would have stayed us here all Day, because it rained very hard, but our Business required more haste, with our Enemies lying so near us. He told us that he could go from his House aboard the Guard-Ship in a Tide's time, and this was the 4th Day since they had seen us. So we marched 3 Miles farther, and then built Huts, where we stayed all Night. It rained all Afternoon, and the greatest Part of the Night.

*

The 4th Day we began our March early, for the Fore-
noons were commonly fair, but there was much rain in
the Afternoon. Though whether it rained or shone it
was much at one with us, for I verily believe we crossed
the Rivers 30 times this Day, the Indians having no
Paths to travel from one part of the Country to another,
and therefore guiding themselves by the Rivers. We
marched this Day 12 Miles, and then built our Hut,
and lay down to sleep. But we always kept two Men
on the Watch, otherwise our own Slaves might have
knocked us on the Head while we slept. It rained
violently all Afternoon, and most of the Night. We
had much ado to kindle a Fire this Evening. Our Huts
were but very mean or ordinary, and our Fire small, so
that we could not dry our Clothes, scarce warm ourselves, and we had no sort of Food for the Belly, all
of which made it very hard with us. I confess these
Hardships quite expelled the Thoughts of an Enemy.
For now, having been 4 Days in the Country, we began
to have but few other Cares than how to get Guides and
Food, and the Spaniards were seldom in our Thoughts.

The 5th Day we set out in the Morning early, and
having travelled 7 Miles in those wild pathless Woods,
by 10 o'clock in the Morning we arrived at a young
Spanish Indian's House, who had formerly lived with
the Bishop of Panama. The young Indian was very
brisk, spoke very good Spanish, and received us very
kindly. This Plantation afforded us store of Provisions,
Yams, and Potatoes, but nothing of any Flesh, besides
2 fat Monkeys we shot, part of which we distributed

25

to some of our Company who were weak and sickly. For others we got Eggs, and such Refreshments as the Indians had, for we still provided for the Sick and Weak. We had a Spanish Indian in our Company, who first took up Arms with Captain Sawkins, and had been with us ever since his Death. He was persuaded to live here by the Master of the House, who promised him his Sister in Marriage, and to be assistant to him in clearing a Plantation. But we would not consent to part from him here, for fear of some Treachery, but promised to release him in two or three Days, when we were certainly out of danger of our Enemies. We stayed here all Afternoon, and dried our Clothes and Ammunition, cleared our Guns, and provided ourselves for a march the next Morning.

Our Surgeon Mr Wafer came to a sad Disaster here. While drying his Powder, a careless Fellow passed by with his Pipe lighted, and set fire to his Powder, which blew up and scorched his Knee, and reduced him to a Condition where he was not able to march. Therefore, we allowed him a Slave to carry his things, being all of us the more concerned at the Accident, because liable ourselves every Moment to Misfortune, and no one to look after us but him. This Indian Plantation was seated on the Bank of the River Congo, in a very fat Soil, and thus far we might have come in our Canoe, if I could have persuaded them to it.

The 6th Day we set out again, having hired another Guide. Here we first crossed the River Congo in a

Canoe, and being over, we marched to the Eastward two Miles, and came to another River, which we forded several Times though it was very deep. Two of our Men were not able to keep Company with us, but came after us as they were able. The last time we forded the River, it was so deep that our tallest Men stood in the deepest Place, and handed over the sick, weak and short Men. By this means we all got over safe, except those two who were behind. Foreseeing a Necessity of wading through Rivers frequently in our Land-march, I took care before I left the Ship to provide myself a large Joint of Bamboo, which I stopped at both Ends, closing it with Wax so as to keep out any Water. In this I preserved my Journal and other Writings from being wet, though I was often forced to swim. When we were over this River, we sat down to wait the coming of our Consorts who were left behind, and in half an Hour they came. But the River by that time was so high that they could not get over it. Nor could we help them over, but only bid them be of good comfort, and stay till the River fell. We marched two Miles farther by the Side of the River, and there built our Huts, having gone this Day six Miles. We had scarce finished our Huts, before the River rose much higher and, overflowing the Banks, obliged us to remove to higher ground. But the next Night came on before we could build more Huts, so we lay straggling in the Woods, some under one Tree, some under another, as we could find convenience, which might have been indifferent comfortable if the Weather had been fair. But the greatest part of the Night we had extraordinary hard Rain, with much Lightning, and terrible Claps of Thunder. These Hardships and Inconveniences made us all careless, and there was no Watch kept (though I believe nobody slept). So our Slaves, taking the Opportunity, went away in the Night; all but one, who was hidden in some hole and knew nothing of their design, or else fell asleep. Those that went away carried with them our Surgeon's gun and all his Money.

The next Morning being the 8th Day, we went to the River's side and found it much fallen. Here our Guide would have us ford it again, which being deep, and the current running swift, we could not. Then we contrived to swim over. Those that could not swim, we were resolved to help over as well as we could. But this was not so feasible, for we should not be able to get all our Things over. At length we concluded to send one Man over with a Line, who should haul over all our Things first, and then get the Men over. This being agreed on, one George Gayny took the end of a Line, made it fast about his Neck, and left the other end ashore, and one Man stood by the Line, to clear it away to him. But when Gayny was in the midst of the Water, the Line, in drawing after him, chanced to kink or grow entangled. The Man standing by to clear it away stopped the Line, which turned Gayny on his back, and he that had the Line in his Hand threw it all into the River after him, thinking he might recover himself. But the Stream running very swift, and the Man having three Hundred Dollars at his Back, he was carried down and never seen again by us. Those two Men whom we left behind the Day before told us afterwards that they found him lying dead in a Creek, where the Eddy had driven him ashore, and the Money on his back. But they had not meddled with any of it, being only in Care how to work their way through a wild unknown Country. This put a Period to that Contrivance. This was the fourth Man that we had lost in this Land-Journey. For the two Men that we had left the Day before did not come to us till we were in the North Seas, so we yielded them also for lost. Being frustrated at getting over the River this way, we looked about for a Tree to fell across the River. At length we found one, which we cut down, and it reached clear over. On this we passed to the other side, where we found a small Plantain Walk, which we soon ransacked.

While we were busy getting Plantains, our Guide was gone, but in less than two Hours he came to us again, and brought with him an old Indian to whom he delivered up his Charge. We gave him a Hatchet and dismissed him, and entered ourselves under the conduct of our new Guide. He immediately led us away, and we crossed another River, entering into a large Valley of the fattest Land I ever took notice of. The Trees were not very thick, but the largest that I saw in all my Travels. We saw great Tracks which were made by the Peccaries, but saw none of them. We marched in this pleasant Country till 3 o'clock in the Afternoon, in all about 4 Miles, and then arrived at the old man's

Country House, which was only a Habitation for hunting. There was a small Plantain walk, some Yams, and Potatoes. Here we took up our Quarters for this Day, and refreshed ourselves with such Food as the place afforded, and dried our Clothes and Ammunition. At this place, our young Spanish Indian provided to leave us, for now we thought ourselves past Danger. This was the Man that was persuaded to stay at the last House we came from, to marry the young Man's Sister. We dismissed him according to our Promise.

The 9th Day the old Man conducted us towards his own Habitation. We marched about 5 Miles in this Valley, and then ascended a Hill, travelling about 5 Miles further over two or three small Hills before we came to any Settlement. Half a mile before we came to the Plantations, we lit upon a Path, which carried us to the Indian Habitations. We saw many wooden Crosses erected in the way, which created some Jealousy in us that here were some Spaniards. Therefore we primed all our Guns anew, and provided ourselves for an Enemy, but coming into the Town found none but Indians, who were all got together in a large House to receive us. For the old Man had a little Boy with him, that he had sent ahead. They made us welcome to what they had, which was very mean, for these were new Plantations, the Corn being not eared. They had no Potatoes, Yams or Plantains, except what they had brought from their old Plantations. There was none of them that spoke good Spanish. Two young Men could speak a little, which caused us to take more notice of them. To these we made a Present, and desired them to get us a Guide to conduct us to the North-side, or part of the way, which they promised to do themselves if we would reward them for it, but told us we must lie still the next Day. Nevertheless, we thought ourselves nearer the North Sea than we were, and proposed to go without a Guide rather than stay here a whole Day. However some of our Men who were tired resolved to stay behind, and Mr Wafer, our Surgeon, who had marched in great Pain ever since his Knee was burned with Powder, resolved to stay with them.

The 10th Day we got up early, resolving to march, but the Indians opposed it as much as they could. Seeing they could not persuade us to stay, however, they came with us, and having taken leave of our friends, we set out.

Here therefore I left the Surgeon and two more, as I said, and marched away to the Eastward following our Guides. We often looked on our Pocket Compasses and showed them to the Guides, pointing at the way that we would go, which made them shake their Heads and say they were pretty Things, but not convenient for us. After we had descended the Hills on which the Town stood, we came down into a Valley, and guided ourselves by a River, which we crossed 22 Times; and having marched 9 Miles, we built Huts and lay there all Night. This Evening I killed a Quaum, a large Bird as big as a Turkey, with which we treated our Guides, for we had brought no Provision with us. This Night our last Slave ran away.

*

William Dampier

The eleventh Day we marched 10 Miles farther, and built Huts at Night, but went supperless to bed.

The twelfth in the Morning we crossed a deep River, passing over it on a Tree, and marched 7 Miles in a low swampy Ground, and came to the side of a great deep River, but could not get over. We built Huts upon its Banks and lay there all Night, upon our Barbecues, or Frames of Sticks, raised about 3 Feet from the Ground.

The thirteenth Day when we turned out, the River had overflown its Banks, and was 2 foot deep in our Huts. Our Guides went from us, not telling us their intent, which made us think they had returned home again. Now we began to repent our haste in coming from the Settlements, for we had had no Food since we came from there. At any rate we found Macaw-berries in this Place, with which we satisfied ourselves this Day, though coarsely.

The fourteenth Day early in the Morning, our Guides came to us again, and the Waters having fallen within their bounds, they carried us to a Tree that stood on the bank of the River, telling us if we could fell that Tree across it, we might pass; if not, we could pass no farther. Therefore we set two of the best Axe-Men that we had, who felled it exactly across the River, and the Boughs just reached over. On this we passed over safe. We afterwards crossed another River three Times, with much Difficulty, and at 3 o'clock in the Afternoon we came to an Indian Settlement, where we met a drove of Monkeys, and killed 4 of them. We stayed here all Night, having marched this Day 6 Miles. Here we got Plantains enough, and a kind reception from the Indian that lived here all alone, except one Boy to wait on him.

The fifteenth Day when we set out, the kind Indian and his Boy went with us in a Canoe, and set us over such Places as we could not ford. And being past those great Rivers, he returned back again, having helped us at least 2 Miles. We marched afterwards 5 Miles, and came to large Plantain-walks, where we took up our Quarters that Night. We there fed plentifully on Plantains, both ripe and green, and had fair Weather all Day and Night. I think these were the largest Plantain-walks, and the biggest Plantains, that I ever saw, but no House near them. We gathered what we pleased by our Guide's Orders.

The sixteenth Day we marched 3 Miles, and came to a large Settlement, where we abode all Day. Not a Man of us did not wish the Journey at an End. Our Feet were blistered, and our Thighs stripped with wading through so many Rivers, the way being almost continually through Rivers, or pathless Woods. In the Afternoon five of us went to seek for Game, and killed 3 Monkeys, which we dressed for Supper. Here we first began to have fair Weather, which continued with us till we came to the North Seas.

*

The eighteenth Day we set out at 10 o'clock, and the Indians, with 5 Canoes, carried us a League up a River; and when we landed the kind Indians went with us and carried our Burdens. We marched 3 Miles farther, and then built our Huts, having travelled from the last Settlements 6 Miles.

The nineteenth Day our Guides lost their way, and we did not march above 2 Miles.

The twentieth Day by 12 o'clock we came to the Cheapo River. The Rivers we crossed hitherto ran all into the South Seas, and the Cheapo was the last we met with that ran that way. Here an old Man, who came from the last Settlements, distributed his burden of Plantains amongst us, and taking his leave returned Home. Afterwards we forded the River, and marched to the foot of a very high Mountain, where we lay all Night. This Day we marched about 9 Miles.

The 21st Day, some of the Indians returned back, and we marched up a very high Mountain. Being on the top, we went some Miles on a ridge, and steep on both sides. We then descended a little, and came to a fine Spring, where we lay all Night, having gone this Day about 9 Miles, the Weather still very fair and clear.

The 22nd Day we marched over another very high Mountain, keeping on the ridge 5 Miles. When we came to the North end, to our great Comfort, we saw the Sea. We descended, and parted ourselves into

3 Companies, and lay by the side of a River, which was the first we met that runs into the North Sea.

The 23rd Day we came through several large Plantain Walks, and at 10 o'clock came to an Indian Habitation, not far from the North Seas. Here we got Canoes to carry us down the River Conception to the Seaside, having gone this Day 7 Miles. We found a great many Indians at the Mouth of the River. They had settled themselves here for the benefit of Trade with the Privateers. Their commodities were Yams, Potatoes, Plantains, Sugar, Canes, Fowls, and Eggs.

The Indians told us that there had been a great many English and French Ships here, which had all gone, except one Barcolongo, a French Privateer, that lay at La Sounds Key. This Island is about 3 Leagues from the Mouth of the River Conception, and is one of the Samballoes, a range of Islands reaching for about 20 Leagues from Point Samballas to Golden Island Eastward. These Islands, or Keys as we call them, were first made the Rendezvous of Privateers in the year 1679, being very convenient for careening, and had Names given to some of them by the Captains of the Privateers; as this La Sounds Key particularly.

Thus we finished our Journey from the South Sea to the North in 23 Days, in which time, by my Account, we travelled 110 Miles, crossing some very high Mountains. But our common March was in the Valleys among deep and dangerous Rivers. At our first landing in this Country, we were told that the Indians were our Enemies. We knew the Rivers to be deep, and the wet season to be coming in. Yet, excepting those we left behind, we lost just one Man, who was drowned, as I said. Our first landing Place on the South Coast was very disadvantageous, for we travelled at least fifty Miles more than we need have done, could we have gone up the Cheapo River, or Santa Maria River. For at either of these Places a man may pass from Sea to Sea in three Days' time with ease. The Indians can do it in a Day and a half, by which you may see how easy it is for a Party of Men to travel over. I must confess the Indians assisted us very much, and I question whether we would have ever got over without their assistance, because they brought us from time to time to their Plantations, where we always got Provision, which otherwise we should have wanted. But if a Party of 500 or 600 Men or more were minded to travel from the North to the South Seas, they may do it without asking leave of the Indians, though it is much better to be Friends with them.

On the 24th of May (having lain one Night at the River's Mouth), we all went on board the Privateer which lay at La Sounds Key. It was a French Vessel, Captain Tristian Commander. The first thing we did was to get such things as we could to gratify our Indian Guides. For we were resolved to reward them to their Heart's content. This we did by giving them Beads, Knives, Scissors and Looking-glasses, which we bought from the Privateers' Crew; and half a Dollar a

Man from each of us. We would have bestowed this in Goods also, but we could not get any, the Privateer having no more Toys. They were so well satisfied with these that they returned with joy to their Friends, and were very kind to our Consorts whom we had left behind, as Mr Wafer our Surgeon and the rest of them told us, when they came to us some Months afterwards.

[. . .]

After extraordinary adventures in North, South and Central America, Dampier crosses the Pacific and reaches Mindanao in the Philippines.

Mindanao Island

While we lay at Guam, we took up a Resolution of going to Mindanao, one of the Philippine Islands, having been told by the Friar and others that it was exceedingly well stored with Provisions, that the Natives were Mahometans, and that they had formerly had a Commerce with the Spaniards, but were now at Wars with them. This Island was therefore thought to be a convenient place for us to go. For besides that, it was on our way to the East Indies, which we had resolved to visit; and the Westerly Monsoon was at hand, which would oblige us to shelter somewhere in a short time, and we could not expect good Harbours in a better place than in so large an Island as Mindanao. Besides all this, I say, the Inhabitants of Mindanao being then, as we were told (though falsely), at Wars with the Spaniards, our Men, who, it should seem, were very squeamish of plundering without Licence, derived hopes of getting a Commission there, from the Prince of the Island, to plunder the Spanish Ships about Manila, and so to make Mindanao their common Rendezvous. And if Captain Swan was minded to go to an English Port, his Men, who thought he intended to leave them, still hoped to get Vessels and Pilots at Mindanao fit for their turn, to cruise on the Coast of Manila. As for Captain Swan, he was willing enough to go there, as best suiting his own design. Therefore this Voyage was concluded on by general consent.

The 21st Day of June we arrived at the Island St John [Siargao Island], which is one of the Philippine Islands. The Philippines are a great company of large Islands, and derive this Name from Phillip II, King of Spain. And even now most of them belong to that Crown.

The chiefest Island in this Range is Luconia [Luzon], which lies on the North of them all. At this Island Magellan died on the Voyage that he was making round the World. For after he had passed those Straits between the South-end of America and Terra del Fuego which now bear his Name, and had ranged down in the South Seas on the back of America, and from there, stretching over to the East Indies, he fell in with the Ladrone Islands. And from there, steering West still, he fell in with these Philippine Islands, and anchored at Luconia, where he warred with the native Indians to bring them in Obedience to his Master the King of Spain, and was killed by them with a poisoned Arrow. It is now wholly under the Spaniards, who have several Towns there. The chief Town is Manila, which is a large Seaport Town near the S.E. end, opposite the Island Mindora. It is a place of great Strength and Trade. The two great Acapulco Ships before-mentioned fetch all sorts of East India Commodities brought here by Foreigners, especially by the Chinese and the Portuguese. Sometimes the English Merchants

of Fort St George send their Ships here, as it were
by stealth, under the charge of Portuguese Pilots and
Mariners. For as yet we cannot get the Spaniards there
to a Commerce with us or the Dutch, although they
have only a few Ships of their own. This seems to arise
from a Jealousy or Fear of discovering the Riches of
these Islands. For most, if not all the Philippine Islands
are rich in Gold, and the Spaniards have no place of
much strength in all these Islands that I ever heard of,
besides Manila itself. Yet they have Villages and Towns
on several of the Islands, and Padres or Priests to instruct
the native Indians, from whom they get their Gold.

The Spanish Inhabitants, especially in the smaller
Islands, would willingly trade with us if the Government was not so severe against them, for they have no
Goods other than what are brought from Manila at an
extraordinarily dear rate. I am of the Opinion that if
any of our Nations were to seek a Trade with them,
they would not lose their labour, for the Spaniards can
and will smuggle as well as any Nation that I know,
and our Jamaica Men are to their profit sensible enough
of it.

There are about 12 or 14 more large Islands lying to the
Southward of Luconia, most of which are inhabited
by the Spaniards. Besides these, there are an infinite
number of small Islands of no account, and even many
of the great Islands are without Names, or at least so
variously set down that I find the same Islands named
by diverse Names.

*

The Islands St John and Mindanao are the southern-most of all these Islands, and are the only Islands in all this Range that are not subject to the Spaniards.

St John's is on the East-side of Mindanao, about 3 or 4 Leagues distant. As we were passing by the S.E. end, we saw a Canoe of Natives under the shore. Therefore one of our Canoes went after her to speak with her, but she ran away from us and, seeing themselves chased, they put their Canoe ashore, leaving her and fleeing into the woods. Nor would they be allured to come to us, although we did what we could to entice them. Besides these Men, we saw no more here, nor any sign of Inhabitants.

When we came aboard our Ship again, we steered away for Mindanao, which was now fair in sight of us, and the 22nd day we came within a League of the east-side and anchored in a small Bay, about a Mile from the Shore, in 10 Fathoms Water, rocky foul Ground.

The Island Mindanao is the biggest of all the Philippine Islands except Luconia. It is a very mountainous Island, full of Hills and Valleys. The Mould in general is deep and black, and extraordinarily fat and fruitful. The sides of the Hills are stony, yet productive enough of very large tall Trees. In the heart of the Country there are some Mountains that yield good Gold. The Valleys are well moistened with pleasant Brooks and small Rivers of delicate Water, and have Trees of several sorts, flourishing and green all the

Year. The Trees are in general very large, and most of them are of kinds unknown to us.

There is one sort which deserves particular notice, called by the Natives Libby-trees. These grow wild in great Groves 5 or 6 Miles long by the sides of the Rivers. Of these Trees Sago is made, which the poor Country People eat instead of Bread 3 or 4 Months in the Year. This Tree, for its Body and Shape, is much like the Palmetto-tree, or the Cabbage-tree, but not so tall as the latter. The Bark and Wood is hard and thin like a Shell, and full of white Pith like that of an Elder. They cut this Tree down, and split it in the middle to scrape out all the Pith, which they beat lustily with a wooden Pestle in a great Mortar or Trough, before putting it into a Cloth or Strainer held over the Trough. Pouring Water in among the Pith, they stir it about in the Cloth, so that the Water carries all the Substance of the Pith through the Cloth down into the Trough, leaving nothing but a light sort of Husk, which they throw away. But what falls into the Trough settles in a short time to the bottom like Mud, and then they draw off the Water and take up the muddy Substance, and make Cakes which, being baked, prove very good Bread.

The Native Indians of Ternate and Tidore, and all the Spice Islands, have plenty of these Trees, and use them for Bread in the same manner. The Sago which is transported to other parts of the East Indies is dried in small pieces like little Seeds or Comfits, and commonly eaten with Milk of Almonds by those that are troubled with the Flux, for it is a great binder, and very good in that Distemper.

In some places of Mindanao there is plenty of Rice, but in the Land they plant Yams, Potatoes and Pumpkins, all of which thrive very well. The other Fruits of this Island arc Water-Melons, Musk-Melons, Plantains, Bananas, Guavas, Nutmegs, Cloves, Betel-Nuts, Durians, Jacks or Jacas, Coco-Nuts, Oranges, &c.

I did not see Nutmeg-trees anywhere, but the Nutmegs this Island produces are fair and large. They have no great store of them, however, being unwilling to propagate them or Cloves, for fear that this should invite the Dutch to visit them and bring them into subjection, as they have done the rest of the neighbouring Islands where they grow. For the Dutch, being seated among the Spice Islands, have monopolised all the Trade into their own Hands, and will not suffer any of the Natives to dispose of it, but to themselves alone. Nay, they are so careful to preserve it in their own Hands, that they will not suffer the Spice to grow in uninhabited Islands, but send Soldiers to cut the Trees down. Captain Rofy told me that while he lived with the Dutch, he had been sent with other Men to cut down the Spice-Trees, and that he himself at several times cut down 7 or 800 Trees. Yet although the Dutch take such care to destroy them, there are many uninhabited Islands that have great plenty of Spice-Trees, as I have been informed by Dutch Men that have been there, particularly by the Captain of a Dutch Ship that I met with at Achin, who told me that near the Island Banda there is an Island where Cloves, falling from the Trees, lie and rot on the ground, and they are, at the time when the Fruit falls, 3 or 4 Inches thick under the Trees. Some others told me that it would not be a hard matter for an English Vessel to purchase a Ship's Cargo of Spice, from the Natives of some of these Spice Islands.

It was a free Merchant who told me this. For by that Name the Dutch and English in the East Indies distinguish those Merchants who are not Servants to the Company. The free Merchants are not suffered to trade to the Spice Islands, nor to many other places where the Dutch have Factories. But they are, on the other Hand, suffered to trade to places where the Dutch Company themselves may not trade, particularly Achin. There are some Princes in the Indies who will not trade with the Company for fear of them. The Seamen that go to the Spice Islands are obliged to bring no Spice from there for themselves, except a small matter for their own use, about a pound or two. Yet the Masters of those Ships commonly so order their business, that they often secure a good quantity, and send it ashore to some place near Batavia before they come into that Harbour (for it is always brought there first before it is sent to Europe). And if they meet any Vessel at Sea that will buy their Cloves, they will sell 10 or 15 Tons out of 100, and yet seemingly carry their Complement to Batavia. For they will pour Water among the remaining part of their Cargo, which will swell them to such a degree that the Ship's Hold will be as full again as it was before any were sold. They use this Trick whenever they dispose of any clandestinely. For when they first take the Cloves in, they are extraordinarily dry, and so will imbibe a great deal of Moisture. This is but one Instance, among many hundreds, of the little deceitful Arts the Dutch Seamen have in these Parts. I believe there are nowhere greater Thieves, and nothing will persuade them to discover one another. For should any do it, the rest would certainly knock him on the Head.

This Island also produces Durians and Jacks. The Trees that bear the Durians are as big as Apple-trees, and full of Boughs. The Rind is thick and rough, and the Fruit so large that they grow only about the Bodies, or on the Limbs near the Body, like the Cacao. The Fruit is about the Bigness of a large Pumpkin, covered with a thick green rough Rind. When it is ripe, the Rind begins to turn yellow, but it is not fit to eat till it opens at the top. Then the Fruit in the inside is ripe, and sends forth an excellent Scent. When the Rind is opened, the Fruit may be split into four quarters. Each quarter has several small Cells that enclose a certain quantity of the Fruit, according to the bigness of the Cell, for some are larger than others. The largest of the Fruit may be as big as a Pullet's Egg. It is as white as Milk, and as soft as Cream, and the Taste very delicious to those that are accustomed to them. But those who have not been used to eating them, will dislike them at first because they smell like roasted

Onions. This Fruit must be eaten in its prime (for there is no eating of it before it is ripe), and even then, it will not keep above a day or two before it putrefies and turns black or a dark colour, and then it is not good. Within the Fruit there is a Stone as big as a small Bean, which has a thin Shell over it. Those that are minded to eat the Stones or Nuts, roast them, and then a thin Shell comes off, which encloses the Nut, and it eats like a Chestnut.

The Jack, or Jaca, is much like the Durian, both in bigness and shape. The Trees that bear them are also much alike, and so is the manner of the Fruit's growing. But the inside is different, for the Fruit of the Durian is white, while that of the Jack is yellow, and fuller of Stones. The Durian is most esteemed, yet the Jack is a very pleasant Fruit, and the Stones or Kernels are good roasted.

There are many other sorts of Grain, Roots and Fruits in this Island which, to give a particular description of, would fill up a large Volume.

On this Island are also many sorts of Beasts, both wild and tame: Horses, Bulls and Cows, Buffaloes, Goats, Wild Hogs, Deer, Monkeys, Guanoes, Lizards, Snakes, &c. I never saw or heard of any Beasts of Prey here, as in many other places. The Hogs are ugly Creatures. They all have great Knobs growing over their Eyes, and there are multitudes of them in the Woods. They are commonly very poor, yet sweet. Deer are very plentiful here in some places, where they are not disturbed.

Of the venomous kinds of Creature, there are Scorpions, whose sting is in their Tail, and Centipedes, called by the English 40 Legs, both of which are also common in the West Indies, in Jamaica and elsewhere. Centipedes are 4 or 5 Inches long, as big as a Goose-Quill, but flattish, of a Dun or reddish colour on the Back, but whitish Belly, and full of Legs on each side of the Belly. Their Sting or Bite is more raging than the Scorpion. They lie in old Houses, and dry Timber. There are several sorts of Snake, some very poisonous. There is another sort of Creature like a Guano, both in colour and shape, but four times as big, whose Tongue is like a small Harpoon, having two beards like the beards of a Fish-hook. It is said to be very venomous, but I do not know its Name. I have seen them in other places also, at the Island Condore and at Achin, and have been told that they are in the Bay of Bengal.

The Fowls of this Country are Ducks and Hens. I have not seen nor heard of any other tame Fowl. The wild Fowl are Pigeons, Parrots, Parakeets, Turtle-Doves, and an abundance of small Fowls. There are Bats as big as a Kite.

The Weather at Mindanao is temperate enough as to heat, for all of it lies so near the Equator; and especially on the borders near the Sea. There they commonly enjoy the Breezes by Day, and cooling Land-Winds at Night. The Winds are easterly one part of the Year, and westerly the other. The easterly Winds begin to blow in October, and it is the middle of November before they are settled. These Winds bring fair Weather. The westerly Winds begin to blow in May, but are not settled till a Month afterwards. The West-Winds always bring Rain, Tornadoes, and very tempestuous Weather. At the first coming in of these Winds they blow faintly. But then the Tornadoes rise one in a Day, sometimes two. These are Thunder-showers which commonly come against the Wind, bringing with them a contrary Wind to what blew before. After the Tornadoes are over, the Wind shifts about again, and the Sky becomes clear, yet then, in the Valleys and the sides of the Mountains, there rises a thick Fog which covers the Land. The Tornadoes continue thus for a Week or more. Then they come thicker, two or three in a Day, bringing violent gusts of Wind, and terrible claps of Thunder. At last, they come so fast that the Wind remains in the Quarter from where these Tornadoes rise, which is out of the West, and there it settles till October or November. When these westward Winds are thus settled, the Sky is all in mourning, being covered with black Clouds and pouring down excessive Rains, sometimes mixed with Thunder and Lightning, that nothing can be more dismal. The Winds rage to such a degree that the biggest Trees are torn up by the Roots, and the Rivers swell and overflow their Banks, and drown the low Land, carrying great

Trees into the Sea. Thus it continues, sometimes a Week together, before the Sun or Stars appear. The fiercest of this Weather is in the latter end of July and in August, for then the Towns seem to stand in a great Pond, and they go from one House to another in Canoes. At this time the Water carries away all the filth and nastiness from under their Houses. Whilst this tempestuous Season lasts, the Weather is cold and chilly. In September the Weather is more moderate, and the Winds are not so fierce, nor the Rain so violent. The Air thenceforward begins to be more clear and delightsome. But then in the Morning there are thick Fogs, continuing till 10 or 11 o'clock before the Sun shines out, especially when it has rained in the Night. In October the easterly Winds begin to blow again and bring fair Weather till April. Thus much concerning the natural state of Mindanao.

[...]

The Turtle

There are 4 sorts of sea Turtle viz. the Trunk-Turtle, the Loggerhead, the Hawksbill and the Green-turtle. The Trunk-Turtle is commonly bigger than the others, their Backs are higher and rounder, and their Flesh rank and not wholesome. The Loggerhead is so called because it has a great head, much bigger than the other sorts. Their flesh is likewise very rank, and seldom eaten but in case of Necessity. They feed on Moss that grows about Rocks. The Hawksbill Turtle is the least kind. They are so called because their Mouths are long and small, somewhat resembling the Bill of a Hawk. On the Backs of these Hawksbill Turtles grows the Shell which is so esteemed for making Cabinets, Combs, and other things. The largest of them may have 3 and a half pounds of Shell. I have taken some that have had 3 pounds 10 Ounces, but they commonly have a pound and a half, or two pounds, some not so much. These are ordinary Food, but generally sweeter than the Loggerhead. Yet in some places, these Hawksbills are unwholesome, causing those that eat them to purge and vomit excessively, especially those between the Samballoes and Portobello.

Hawksbill Turtles are in many places of the West Indies. They have Islands and places peculiar to themselves, where they lay their Eggs, and seldom come among any other Turtle. These and all other Turtles lay Eggs in the Sand. Their Time of laying is in May, June, and July. Some begin sooner, some later. They lay 3 times in a Season, and at each Time 80 or 90 Eggs. Their Eggs are as big as a Hen's Egg, and very round, covered only with a white, tough Skin. There are some Bays on the North-side of Jamaica, where these Hawksbills resort to lay. In the Bay of Honduras are Islands which they likewise make their breeding places, and many places all along the Coast on the Main of the West Indies, from Trinidado to La Vera Cruz, in the Bay of Nova Hispania.

When a Sea-turtle returns out of the Sea to lay, she is at least an Hour before she returns again, for she has to go above High-water Mark, and if it is low Water when she comes ashore, she must rest once or twice, being heavy, before she comes to the place where she lays. When she has found a place for her purpose, she makes a great Hole with her Fins in the Sand, in which she lays her Eggs, then covers them 2 feet deep with the same Sand that she threw out of the Hole, and so returns. Sometimes they come up the Night before they intend to lay, and take a view of the place, and so having made a Tour or semi-circular March, they return to the Sea again, and never fail to come ashore the next Night to lay near that place. All sorts of Turtle use the same methods in laying.

*

The Green-turtles are so called because their Shell is greener than any other. It is very thin and clear, and better clouded than the Hawksbill, but it is used only for inlays, being extraordinarily thin. These Turtles are generally larger than the Hawksbill, weighing 2 or 3 hundred Pounds. Their Backs are flatter than the Hawksbill, their Heads round and Small. Green-turtles are the sweetest of all the kinds, but there are degrees of them, both in respect to their Flesh and their bigness. I have observed that, at Blanco in the West Indies, the Green-turtle (which is the only kind there) are larger than any other in the North Seas. There they will commonly weigh 280 or 300 pounds. Their Fat is yellow, and the Lean white, and their Flesh extraordinarily sweet. At Boccatoro, West of Portobello, they are not so large, their Flesh not so white, nor the fat so yellow. Those in the Bay of Honduras and Campeachy are somewhat smaller still. Their fat is green, and the lean of a darker colour than those at Boccatoro. I heard of a monstrous Green-turtle once taken at Port Royal in the Bay of Campeachy that was four Feet deep from the Back to the Belly, and the Belly six feet broad. Capt. Roch's Son, of about nine or ten Years of Age, went in it as in a Boat, on board his Father's Ship, about a quarter of a Mile from the Shore. The leaves of Fat afforded eight Gallons of Oil. The Turtles that live among the Keys, on the South-side of Cuba, are a mixed sort, some bigger, some less, and so their Flesh is of a mixed Colour, some green, some dark, some yellowish. Port Royal in Jamaica is constantly supplied with these, by Sloops that come here with

Nets to take them. They carry them alive to Jamaica, where the Turtles have Wires made with Stakes in the Sea, to preserve them alive. The Market is plentifully stored with Turtle every Day, it being the common Food there, chiefly for the ordinary sort of People.

There is another sort of Green-turtle in the South Seas which are small, yet pretty sweet. These lie Westward on the Coast of Mexico. A thing very strange and remarkable in these Creatures, is that, at the breeding Time, they leave their common haunts for two or three Months, where they feed most of the Year, and resort to other Places only to lay their Eggs. And it is not thought that they eat anything during this Season, so that both the He's and She's grow very lean, but the He's to such a degree that none will eat them. The most remarkable Places that I ever heard of for their breeding is at an Island in the West Indies called Caimanes, and the Isle Ascension in the Western Ocean. And when the breeding Time is past, there are none remaining. Doubtless they swim some hundreds of Leagues to come to those two Places, for it has often been observed that at Caimanes, in the breeding Time, there are found all those sorts of Turtle before-described. The South Keys of Cuba are more than 40 Leagues from there, which is the nearest Place that these Creatures can come from, and it is most certain that there could not live so many there as come here in one Season.

*

Those that go to lay at Ascension, must needs travel much farther, for there is no Land nearer than 300 Leagues, and it is certain that these Creatures always live near the Shore. In the South Seas likewise, the Gallapagos is the place where they live the biggest part of the Year. Yet they go from there, at their Season, over to the Main to lay their Eggs, which is 100 Leagues to the nearest Place. Although Multitudes of these Turtles go from their common Places of feeding and abode to these laying Places, they do not all go. And at the Time when the Turtle resort to these Places to lay their Eggs, they are accompanied with abundance of Fish, especially Sharks. For the Places which the Turtles then leave are destitute of Fish, which follow the Turtles.

When the She's go thus to their places to lay, the Males accompany them, and never leave them till they return. Both Males and Females are fat at the beginning of the Season. But before they return, the Males, as I said, are so lean that they are not fit to eat, but the Females are good to the very last, yet not so fat as at the beginning of the Season. It is reported of these Creatures that they are nine Days engendering, in the Water, the Male on the Female's Back. It is observable that the Males, while engendering, do not easily forsake their Female. I have gone and taken hold of the Male when engendering, and a very bad Striker may strike them then, for the Male is not shy at all. But the Females, seeing a Boat when they rise to blow, would make her escape, except that the Male grips her with his two fore-Fins and holds her fast. When they are thus coupled, it is best to strike the Female first, and then you are sure of the Male also. These Creatures are thought to live to a great Age, and it is observed by the Jamaica Turtlers that they are many Years before they come to their full Growth.

[...]

The Sucking-fish

The Sucking-fish is about the bigness of a large Whiting, and of much the same make towards the Tail, but the Head is flatter. From the Head to the middle of its Back, there grows a sort of Flesh, of a hard gristly Substance, like that of the Limpet (a Shell-fish tapering up pyramidically) which sticks to the Rocks; or like the Mouth of a Shell-Snail, but harder. This Excrescence is of a flat and oval form, about seven or eight Inches long, and five or six broad, rising about half an Inch high. It is full of small Ridges with which it will fasten itself to anything that it meets with in the Sea, just as a Snail does to a Wall.

When any of them happen to come about a ship, they seldom leave her, for they will feed on such Filth as is daily thrown overboard, or on mere Excrements. When it is fair Weather and little Wind, they will play about the ship. But in blustering Weather, or when the Ship sails quick, they commonly fasten themselves to the Ship's Bottom, from where neither the Ship's Motion, though never so swift, nor the most tempestuous Sea can remove them. They will likewise fasten themselves to any other bigger Fish, for they never swim fast themselves, if they meet with anything to carry them. I have found them sticking to a Shark, after it was hauled in on the Deck, though a Shark is so strong and boisterous a Fish, and throws about him so vehemently for half an Hour when caught, that, if the Sucking Fish did not stick at no ordinary rate, it would be cast off by so much Violence.

It is also usual to see them sticking to Turtles, to any old Trees, Planks, or the like, that lie driven at Sea. Any Knobs or Inequalities on a Ship's Bottom are a great Hindrance to the Swiftness of its sailing, and 10 or 12 of these sticking to it must needs retard it, as much, in a manner, as if its Bottom were foul. So that I am inclined to think that this Fish is the Remora, of which the Ancients tell such Stories. If it is not, I know no other that is, and I leave the Reader to judge. I have seen these Sucking-fishes in great plenty in the Bay of Campeachy, and in all the Sea between that and the Coast of Caraccos, particularly about the Islands Rocas, Blanco, Tortugas, &c. They have no Scales, and are very good Meat.

[. . .]

The Manatee

I have seen the Manatee in the Bluefields River, in the Bay of Campeachy, on the Coasts of Bocca del Drago and Boccatoro, in the River of Darien, and among the South Keys of Cuba. I have heard of a few being found on the North of Jamaica, and great Multitudes in the Rivers of Surinam, which is very low Land. I have also seen them at Mindanao, one of the Philippine Islands, and on the Coast of New Holland.

This Creature is about the Bigness of a Horse, and 10 or 12 Feet long. The Mouth of it is much like the Mouth of a Cow, having great thick Lips. The Eyes are no bigger than a small Pea. The Ears are only two small holes on each side of the Head. The Neck is short and thick, bigger than the Head. The biggest Part of this Creature is at the Shoulders, where it has two large Fins, one on each side of its Belly. Under each of these Fins the Female has a small Dug to suckle her Young. From the Shoulders towards the Tail it retains its bigness for about a Foot, then grows smaller and smaller to the very Tail, which is flat, and about 14 Inches broad, 20 Inches long, and in the Middle 4 or 5 Inches thick, but no more than 2 Inches thick about the Edges of it. From the Head to the Tail it is round and smooth, without any Fin except the two before mentioned. I have heard that some have weighed above 1200 pounds, but I never saw any so large.

The Manatee delights to live in brackish Water and they are commonly in Creeks and Rivers near the Sea. It is for this Reason, possibly, that they are not seen in the South Seas (that I could ever observe), where the Coast is generally a bold Shore, that is high Land and deep Water close by it, with a high Sea or great Surges. Whereas the West Indies, being as it were, one great Bay composed of many smaller ones, are mostly low Land and shallow Water, and afford proper Pasture (as I may say) for the Manatee. Sometimes we find them in Salt-Water, sometimes in fresh, but never far at Sea. And those that live in the Sea at such Places where there is no River or Creek fit for them to enter, commonly come once or twice in 24 Hours to the Mouth of any Fresh-Water River that is near their Place of Abode.

They live on Grass 7 or 8 Inches long, and of a narrow Blade, which grows in the Sea in many places, especially among Islands near the Main. This Grass grows likewise in Creeks, or near the Sides of great Rivers, in such places where there is little Tide or Current. They never come ashore, nor into Water shallower than where they can swim. Their Flesh is white, both the Fat and the Lean, and extraordinarily sweet, wholesome Meat. The Tail of a young Cow is most esteemed, but if old, both Head and Tail are very tough. A Calf that sucks is the most delicate Meat. Privateers commonly roast them, as they also do great pieces cut out of the Bellies of the old ones.

The Skin of the Manatee is of great use to Privateers, for they cut them into Straps, which they make fast on the Sides of their Canoes, and through which they put their oars in rowing. The Skin of the Bull, or of the Back of the Cow, is too thick for this use, but they make Horse-whips from this, cutting them 2 or 3 Feet long. At the Handle they leave the full Substance of the Skin, and from there, cut it away tapering, but very even and square all four Sides. While the Thongs are green, they wist them and hang them to dry. In a Week's time these become as hard as Wood.

The Moskito Men always have a small Canoe at their disposal to strike Fish, Tortoise or Manatee, which they usually keep to themselves, and very neat and clean. They use no Oars, but Paddles, the broad Part of which does not go tapering towards the Staff, as in the Oar. Nor do they use it in the same manner, laying it on the Side of the Vessel, but hold it perpendicular, gripping the Staff hard with both Hands, and putting back the Water by main Strength and very quick Strokes. One of the Moskitos (for they go but two in a Canoe) sits in the Stern. The other kneels down at the Head, and both paddle till they come to the Place where they expect their Game. Then they lie still, or paddle very softly, looking well about them, and the Man at the Head of the Canoe lays down his Paddle, and stands up with his striking Staff in his Hand.

*

This Staff is about 8 Feet long, almost as big as a Man's Arm at the great End, in which there is a Hole to place his Harpoon in. At the other end of his Staff there is a piece of light Wood called Bobwood, with a Hole in it, through which the small End of the Staff comes. And on this piece of Bobwood, there is a Line of 10 or 12 Fathoms wound neatly about, and the End of the Line made fast to it. The other End of the Line is made fast to the Harpoon, which is at the great End of the Staff, and the Moskito Men keep about a Fathom of it loose in their Hands. When he strikes, the Harpoon presently comes out of the Staff, and, as the Manatee swims away, the Line runs off from the Bob, and although at first both Staff and Bob may be carried under Water, it will rise again as the Line runs off. Then the Mosquito Men paddle with all their might to get hold of the Bob again, and usually spend a quarter of an Hour before they get it. When the Manatee begins to be tired, it lies still, and then the Moskito Men paddle to the Bob and take it up, and begin to haul in the Line. When the Manatee feels them he swims away again, with the Canoe after him. Then the Steersman must be nimble to turn the Head of the Canoe the way that his Consort points, who being in the Head of the Canoe, and holding the Line, both sees and feels which way the Manatee is swimming. Thus the Canoe is towed with a violent Motion, till the Manatee's Strength decays. Then they gather in the Line, which they are often forced to let all go to the very End. At length, when the Creature's Strength is spent, they haul it up to the Canoe's side, knocking it on the Head, and towing it to the nearest Shore, where they make it fast and seek for another; which having taken, they get on shore with it to put it into their Canoe. For it is so heavy that they cannot lift it in, but they haul it up in shallow Water, as near the Shore as they can, and then overset the Canoe, laying one side close to the Manatee. Then they roll it in, which brings the Canoe upright again, and when they have heaved out the Water, they fasten a line to the other Manatee that lies afloat, and tow it after them.

I have known two Moskito Men every Day for a Week bring aboard 2 Manatee in this manner, the least of which has not weighed less than 600 Pounds, and that in a very small Canoe, which three Englishmen would scarce adventure to go in. When they strike a Cow that has a young one, they seldom miss the Calf, for she commonly takes her Young under one of her Fins. But if the Calf is so big that she cannot carry it, or so frightened that she only minds to save her own Life, the Young will never leave her till the Moskito Men have had an opportunity to strike her.

[. . .]

Flying Foxes near Negros Island

In the Middle of this Bay, about a Mile from the Shore, there is a small low woody Island, not above a Mile in Circumference: our Ship rode about a Mile from it. This Island was the Habitation of an incredible Number of great Bats, with Bodies as big as Ducks, or large Fowl, and with vast Wings: for I saw at Mindanao one of this Sort, and I judge that the Wings stretched out in length, could not be less asunder than seven or eight foot from Tip to Tip; for it was much more than any of us could fathom with our Arms extended to the Utmost. The Wings are for Substance like those of other Bats, of a dun or mouse Colour. The Skin or Leather of them has Ribs running along it, and draws up in three or four Folds; and at the Joints of those Ribs and the Extremities of the Wings, there are sharp and crooked Claws, by which they may hang on Anything. In the Evening as soon as the Sun was set, these Creatures would begin to take their Flight from this Island, in swarms like Bees, directing their Flight over to the main Island; and whither afterwards I know not. Thus we should see them rising up from the Island till Night hindered our Sight; and in the Morning as soon as it was light, we should see them returning again like a Cloud, to the small Island, till sunrising. This Course they kept constantly while we lay here, affording us every Morning and Evening an hour's Diversion in gazing at them, and talking about them; but our Curiosity did not prevail with us to go ashore to them, ourselves and Canoes being all the daytime taken up in Business about our Ship. At this Isle also we found plenty of Turtle and Manatee, but no Fish.

[...]

New Holland

The 4th Day of January 1688 we fell in with the Land of New Holland [Australia] in the Lat. of 16d. 50m. We ran in close by it, and finding no convenient anchoring, because it lies open to the N.W., we ran along the shore to the Eastward, steering N.E. by E., for so the Land lies. We steered thus about 11 Leagues, and then came to a Point of Land from where the Land trends East and southerly for 10 or 12 Leagues, but how afterwards, I do not know. About 3 Leagues to the eastward of this Point there is a pretty deep Bay with an abundance of Islands in it, and a very good place to anchor in or to haul ashore. About a League to the eastward of that Point, we anchored January the 5th 1688, two Miles from the Shore in 19 Fathoms, good hard Sand and clean Ground.

New Holland is a very large Tract of Land. It is not yet determined whether it is an Island or a main Continent, but I am certain that it joins neither to Asia, Africa nor America. The part of it that we saw is all low, even Land with sandy Banks against the Sea. Only the Points are rocky, and so are some of the Islands in this Bay.

*

The Land is of a dry sandy Soil, destitute of Water except you make Wells, yet producing diverse sorts of Trees. But the Woods are not thick, nor the Trees very big. Most of the Trees that we saw are Dragon-Trees as we supposed, and these too are the largest Trees of any there. They are about the bigness of our large Apple-trees and about the same height, and the Rind is blackish and somewhat rough. The Leaves are of a dark Colour. Gum distils out of the Knots or Cracks that are in the Bodies of the Trees. We compared it with some Gum-Dragon, or Dragon's Blood, that was aboard, and it was of the same colour and taste. The other sorts of Tree were not known by any of us. There was pretty long Grass growing under the Trees but it was very thin. We saw no Trees that bore Fruit or Berries.

We saw no sort of Animal, nor any Tracks of Beasts but once, and that seemed to be the Tread of a Beast as big as a great Mastiff Dog. There are a few small Land-birds, but none bigger than a Blackbird, and but few Sea-fowls. Nor is the Sea very plentifully stored with Fish unless you reckon the Manatee and Turtle as such. Of these Creatures there is plenty, but they are extraordinarily shy, though the Inhabitants cannot trouble them much, having neither Boats nor Iron.

The Inhabitants of this Country are the miserablest People in the World. The Hodmadods of Mono-matapa, though a nasty People, yet for Wealth are Gentlemen to these. They have no Houses, or skin

Garments, Sheep, Poultry, Fruits of the Earth, Ostrich Eggs, &c., as the Hodmadods have. And setting aside their Human Shape, they differ little from Brutes. They are tall, straight-bodied and thin, with small long Limbs. They have great Heads, round Foreheads, and great Brows. Their Eyelids are always half closed, to keep the Flies out of their Eyes, they being so trouble-some here that no fanning will keep them from coming to one's Face. And without the Assistance of both Hands to keep them off, they will creep into one's Nostrils, and Mouth too, if the Lips are not shut very close. So being thus annoyed with these Insects from their Infancy, they never open their Eyes as other People, and therefore cannot see far unless they hold up their Heads, as if they were looking at something over them.

They have great Bottle-Noses, pretty full Lips and wide Mouths. The two Fore-teeth of their Upper-jaw are wanting in all of them, Men and Women, old and young. Whether they draw them out I do not know. Nor have they any Beards. They are long-visaged and of a very unpleasing Aspect, having no one graceful Feature in their Faces. Their Hair is black, short and curled like that of the Negroes, and not long and lank like the common Indians. The Colour of their Skins, both of their Faces and the rest of their Body is Coal-black like that of the Negroes of Guinea.

They have no sort of Clothes but a piece of the Rind of a Tree, tied like a Girdle about their Waists, and a handful of long Grass, or three or four small green Boughs full of Leaves thrust under their Girdle, to cover their Nakedness.

They have no Houses but lie in the open Air without any covering, the Earth being their Bed and the Heaven their Canopy. Whether they cohabit, one Man to one Woman or promiscuously, I do not know, but they do live in Companies of 20 or 30 Men, Women and Children together. Their only Food is a small sort of Fish, which they get by making Wares of Stone across little Coves or Branches of the Sea. Every Tide brings in the small Fish and leaves them there for Prey to these People, who constantly attend to search for them at Low-water. This small Fry I take to be the top of their Fishery. They have no Instruments to catch great Fish, should they come and (rarely) be left behind at Low-water. Nor could we catch any Fish with our Hooks and Lines all the while we lay there. In other Places at Low-water they seek Cockles, Mussels and Periwinkles. There are fewer still of these Shellfish, so that their chiefest dependence is upon what the Sea leaves in their Wares. Whether this is much or little, they gather it up and march to the Places of their Abode. There the old People that are not able to stir abroad by reason of their Age, and the tender Infants, wait their return. And what Providence has bestowed on them, they presently broil on the Coals and eat it in common. Sometimes they get as many Fish as makes them a plentiful Banquet, and at other times they scarce get every one a taste. But whether they get little or much, every one has his part, the young and tender as well as the old and feeble, who are not able to go abroad as can the strong and lusty. When they have eaten, they lie down till the next Low-water, and then all who are able march out, be it Night or Day, rain or shine: it is all one. They must attend the Wares or else they must fast, for the Earth affords them no Food at all. There is neither Herb, Root, Pulse, nor any sort of Grain for them to eat, that we saw, nor any sort of Bird or Beast that they can catch, having no Instruments with which to do so.

I did not perceive that they did worshipped anything. These poor Creatures have a sort of Weapon to defend their Ware or fight with their Enemies, if there are any that will interfere with their poor Fishery. At first they endeavoured to frighten us with their Weapons, since lying ashore, we had deterred them from one of their Fishing-places. Some of them had wooden Swords, others had a sort of Lance. The Sword is a piece of Wood shaped somewhat like a Cutlass. The Lance is a long strait Pole, sharp at one end and hardened afterwards by heat. I saw no Iron, nor any other sort of Metal. Therefore it is probable they use Stone-Hatchets, as do some Indians in America.

How they get their Fire, I do not know, but probably as Indians do, out of Wood. I have seen the Indians of Bon-Airy do it, and have myself tried the Experiment. They take a flat piece of Wood that is pretty soft, and make a small dent in one side of it. Then they take another hard round Stick about the bigness of one's little Finger, and sharpening it at one end like a Pencil, they put that sharp end in the hole or dent of the flat soft piece, and then rubbing or twirling the hard piece between the Palms of their Hands, they drill the soft piece till it smokes and at last takes Fire.

These People speak somewhat through the Throat, but we could not understand one word that they said. We anchored, as I said before, January the 5th, and seeing Men walking on the Shore, we presently sent a Canoe to get some Acquaintance with them, for we were in hopes to get some Provision among them. But the Inhabitants, seeing our Boat coming, ran away and hid themselves. We searched afterwards three Days in hopes to find their Houses, but found none. Yet we saw many places where they had made Fires. At last, being out of hopes to find their Habitations, we searched no farther but left a great many Toys ashore in such places where we thought that they would come. In all our search we found no Water, but old Wells on the sandy Bays.

At last we went over to the Islands, and there we found a great many of the Natives. I believe there were 40 on one Island, Men, Women and Children. The Men, at our first coming ashore, threatened us with their Lances and Swords, but they were frightened by a Gun, which we fired purposely to scare them. The Island was so small that they could not hide themselves. But they were greatly disordered at our Landing, especially the Women and Children, for we went directly to their Camp. The lustiest of the Women, snatching up their Infants, ran away howling and the little Children ran after, squeaking and bawling. But the Men stood still. Some of the Women, and such People as could not go from us, lay still by a Fire, making a doleful noise, as if we had been coming to devour them. But when they saw we did not intend to harm them, they were pretty quiet, and the rest that had fled from us at our first coming returned again. This Dwelling place of theirs was only a Fire, with a few Boughs before it, set up on the side the Wind was from.

After we had been here a little while, the Men began to be familiar and we clothed some of them, designing to have some service from them. For we had found some Wells of Water here and intended to carry 2 or 3 Barrels of it aboard. But as it was somewhat troublesome to carry it to the Canoes, we thought to have got these Men to carry it for us. And therefore we gave them some old Clothes: to one, an old pair of Breeches; to another, a ragged Shirt; to the third, a Jacket that was scarce worth owning, which would have been very acceptable at some places where we had been. And so we thought they might have been acceptable with these People. We put them on them, thinking that this finery would have brought them to work heartily for us. And having filled our Water in small long Barrels, about six Gallons in each, which were made purposely to carry Water in, we brought our new Servants to the Wells, and put a Barrel on each of their Shoulders for them to carry to the Canoe. But all the signs we could make were to no purpose, for they stood like Statues without motion, and grinned like so many Monkeys, staring one upon another. For these poor Creatures do not seem accustomed to carrying Burdens, and I believe that one of our Ship-boys of 10 Years old would carry as much as one of them. So we were forced to carry our Water ourselves. They very fairly put the Clothes off again, and laid them down as if Clothes were only for working in. I did not perceive that they had any great liking for them at first. Nor did they seem to admire anything that we had.

At another time our Canoe, seeking Game among these Islands, espied a drove of these Men swimming from one Island to another. For they have no Boats, Canoes or Bark-logs. They took up Four of them and brought them aboard. Two of them were middle-aged. The other two were young Men, about 18 or 20 Years old. To these we gave boiled Rice, and with it boiled Turtle and Manatee. They greedily devoured what we gave them, but took no notice of the Ship or anything in it, and when they were set on Land again, they ran away as fast as they could. At our first coming, before we were acquainted with them, or they with us, a Company of them who lived on the Main came just against our Ship, and standing on a pretty high Bank, threatened us with their Swords and Lances by shaking them at us. At last the Captain ordered the Drum to be beaten, which was done of a sudden with much vigour, purposely to scare the poor Creatures. Hearing the noise, they ran away as fast as they could drive. And when they ran away in haste, they would cry *Gurry, Gurry*, speaking deep in the Throat. Those Inhabitants who live on the Main would always run away from us, yet we took several of them. For, as I have already observed, they had such bad Eyes that they could not see us till we came close to them. We always gave them Victuals and let them go again, but the Islanders, after our first time among them, did not stir for us.

When we had been here about a Week we hauled our Ship into a small sandy Cove, at a Spring-tide, as far as she would float. And at low Water she was left dry, with the Sand around us dry for nearly half a Mile. For the Sea rises and falls here about five Fathoms. The Flood runs North by East, and the Ebb South by West. All the Neap-tides we lay wholly aground, for the Sea did not come near us by about a hundred Yards. We therefore had time enough to clean our Ship's bottom, which we did very well. Most of our Men lay ashore in a Tent, where our Sails were mending, and our Strikers brought home Turtle and Manatee every Day, which was our constant Food.

While we lay here I endeavoured to persuade our Men to go to some English Factory, but was threatened to be turned ashore and left here for it. This made me desist, and patiently wait for some more convenient place and opportunity to leave them than here. I hoped I should accomplish this in a short time, because they intended, after leaving here, to bear down towards Cape Comorin. On their way there they also designed to visit the Island Cocos, which lies in Lat. 12d. 12m. North by our Drafts, hoping to find there some of that Fruit, the Island having its Name from these.

After reaching the Nicobar Islands Dampier and a few companions remain there after their ship leaves. They then attempted to sail a small boat to Achin [Banda Aceh] in northern Sumatra.

From Nicobar to Sumatra in an Open Boat

It was the 15th Day of May 1688, about four o'clock in the Afternoon, when we left Nicobar Island directing our Course towards Achin, being eight Men of us in Company, viz. three English, four Malayans who were born at Achin, and the mongrel Portuguese.

Our Vessel, the Nicobar Canoe, was not one of the biggest, nor of the least size. She was much about the Burden of one of our London Wherries below Bridge, and built sharp at both ends like the forepart of a Wherry. She was deeper than a Wherry but not so broad, and was so thin and light that, when empty, four Men could launch her or haul her ashore on a sandy Bay. We had a good substantial Mast and a Mat Sail, and good Outlayers lashed very fast and firm on each side, the Vessel being made of strong Poles. While these continued firm, the Vessel could not overset, which she would easily have done without them, and with them too, had they not been made very strong. We were therefore much beholding to our Achinese Companions for this Contrivance.

These Men were none of them so sensible of the Danger as Mr Hall and myself, for they all confided so much in us, that they did not so much as scruple anything that we approved of. Nor was Mr Hall so well provided as I was. For before we left the Ship, I had purposely consulted our Draft of the East Indies (for we had but one in the Ship), and out of that, I had written in my Pocketbook an account of the bearing and distance of all the Malacca Coast, and that of Sumatra, Pegu and Siam, and also brought away with me a Pocket Compass for my Direction in any Enterprise that I should undertake.

The Weather at our setting out was very fair, clear and hot. The Wind was still at S.E., a very small Breeze just fanning the Air, and the Clouds moving gently from West to East, which gave us hopes that the Winds were either at West, already abroad at Sea, or would be so in a very short time. We took this Opportunity of fair Weather, being in hopes to accomplish our Voyage to Achin before the western Monsoon was set in strong, knowing that we should have very blustering Weather after this fair Weather, especially at the first coming of the western Monsoon.

We rowed therefore away to the Southward, supposing that when we were clear from the Island, we should have a true Wind, as we call it, for the Land draws in the Wind, and we often find the Wind at Sea different from what it is near the Shore. We rowed with four Oars, taking our turns. Mr Hall and I also steered by turns, for none of the rest were capable of it. We rowed the first Afternoon and the Night ensuing about twelve Leagues by my Judgement. Our Course was South-

South-East, but the 16th Day in the Morning, when the Sun was an Hour high, we saw the Island from where we had come, bearing N.W. by N. Therefore I found we had gone a point more to the East than I intended, for which reason we steered S. by E.

In the Afternoon at 4 o'clock, we had a gentle Breeze at W.S.W., which continued so till nine, all of which time we laid down our Oars and steered away S.S.E. I was then at the Helm, and I found by the rippling of the Sea that there was a strong Current against us. It made a great noise that might be heard for nearly half a Mile. At 9 o'clock it fell calm and so continued till ten. Then the Wind sprang up again and blew a fresh Breeze all Night.

The 17th Day in the Morning we looked out for the Island Sumatra, supposing that we were now within 10 Leagues of it, for we had rowed and sailed by our reckoning 24 Leagues from Nicobar Island, and the distance from Nicobar to Achin is about 40 Leagues. But we looked in vain for the Island Sumatra, and turning ourselves about, we saw to our Grief Nicobar Island lying W.N.W., and not above eight Leagues distant. By this, it was visible that we had met a very strong Current against us in the Night. But the Wind freshened on us and we made the best use of it while the Weather continued fair. At Noon we had an Observation of the Sun. My lat. was 6d. 55m., and Mr Hall's was 7d. N.

*

The 18th Day the Wind freshened on us again and the Sky began to be clouded. It was indifferent clear till Noon and we thought to have had an Observation, but we were hindered by the Clouds that covered the Face of the Sun when it came on the Meridian. We also then had a very ill Presage, by a great Circle about the Sun five or six times the Diameter of it, which seldom appears without storms of Wind or much Rain ensuing. Such Circles about the Moon are more frequent but of less import. We commonly take great notice of those that are about the Sun, observing if there is any Breach in the Circle, and in what Quarter the Breach is. From there we commonly find the greatest Stress of the Wind will come. I must confess that I was a little anxious at the Sight of this Circle, and wished heartily that we were near some Land. Yet I showed no sign of it to discourage any Consorts, but made a Virtue of Necessity, and put a good Countenance on the Matter.

I told Mr Hall that if the Wind became too strong and violent, as I feared it would, it being even then very strong, we must of necessity steer away before the Wind and Sea till better Weather presented; and that as the Winds were now, we should, instead of about twenty Leagues to Achin, be driven sixty or seventy Leagues to the Coast of Cudda or Queda, a Kingdom, Town and Harbour of Trade on the Coast of Malacca.

The Winds therefore being very hard, we rolled up the Foot of our Sail on a Pole fastened to it, and settled our Yard within three Feet of the Canoe's sides, so that we had now but a small Sail. Yet it was still too big, considering the Wind. For the Wind, being on our Broad-side, pressed her down very much, though supported by her Outlayers. So much so that the Poles of the Outlayers going from the Sides of their Vessel bent, as if they would break. And should they have broken, our overturning and perishing would have been inevitable. Besides, the increasing Sea would soon have filled the Vessel this way. Yet we made a shift to bear up with the side of the Vessel against the Wind for a while. But the Wind still increasing, about One o'clock in the Afternoon we put away right before Wind and Sea, continuing to run thus all the Afternoon and part of the Night ensuing. The Wind continued increasing all the Afternoon and the Sea swelled higher still, and often broke, but did us no damage, for the Ends of the Vessel being very narrow, he that steered received and broke the Sea on his Back, and so kept it from coming in so much as to endanger the Vessel. Nevertheless, much Water would come in, which we were forced continually to keep heaving out. And by this time we saw it was well that we had altered our Course, else every wave would have filled and sunk us, taking the side of the Vessel. And though our Outlayers were well lashed down to the Canoe's Bottom with Rattans, they probably would have yielded to such a Sea as this, when even beforehand they had been plunged under Water and bent like Twigs.

*

The Evening of this 18th Day was very dismal. The Sky looked very black, being covered with dark Clouds, the Wind blew hard, and the Seas ran high. The Sea was already roaring in a white Foam about us. A dark Night was coming on, there was no Land in sight to shelter us, and our little Ark was in danger of being swallowed by every Wave. And, what was worst of all, none of us thought ourselves prepared for another World. The Reader may better guess than I can express the Confusion that we were all in. I had been in many imminent Dangers before now, some of which I have already related, but the worst of them all was but a Play-game in comparison with this. I must confess that I was in great Conflicts of Mind at this time. Other Dangers did not come upon me with such a leisurely and dreadful Solemnity. A sudden Skirmish or Engagement, or so, was nothing when one's Blood was up, and pushed forwards with eager Expectations. But here I had a lingering View of approaching Death, and little or no hopes of escaping it. And I must confess that my Courage, which I had hitherto kept up, failed me here, and I made very sad Reflections on my former Life, looking back with Horror and Detestation on Actions which before I disliked, but now trembled at the remembrance of. I had long before this repented of that roving Course of Life, but never with such Concern as now. I also called to mind the many miraculous Acts of God's Providence towards me in the whole Course of my Life, of which kind I believe few Men have met with the like. For all these I returned Thanks in a peculiar Manner, and once more desired

God's Assistance, composing my Mind as well as I could in the Hopes of it, and, as the Event showed I was not disappointed of my Hopes.

Submitting ourselves therefore to God's good Providence, and taking all the Care we could to preserve our Lives, Mr Hall and I took turns to steer, and the rest took turns to heave out the Water. And thus we provided to spend the most doleful Night I was ever in. About Ten o'clock it began to thunder, lightening and rain, but the Rain was very welcome to us, as we had drunk up all the Water we brought from the Island.

The Wind at first blew harder than before, but within half an Hour it abated and became more moderate, and the Sea also assuaged its Fury. By a lit Match, of which we kept a Piece burning on purpose, we looked on our Compass to see how we had steered, and found our Course to be still East. We had had no occasion to look on the Compass before, for we had steered right before the Wind, which, if it had shifted, we would have been obliged to alter accordingly. But it now being abated, we found our Vessel lively enough with the small Sail then aboard, to haul to our former Course S.S.E., which accordingly we did, being now in hopes again to get to the Island Sumatra.

But about Two o'clock in the Morning of the 19th Day, we had another Gust of Wind with much Thunder, Lightning and Rain. This lasted till Day, and obliged us to put before the Wind again, steering thus for several Hours. It was very dark, and the hard Rain soaked us so thoroughly that we had not one dry Thread about us. The Rain chilled us extremely, for any fresh Water is much colder than that of the Sea. Even in the coldest Climates, the Sea is warm; and in the hottest Climates, the Rain is cold and unwholesome for Man's Body. In this wet starveling's Plight we spent the tedious Night. Never did poor Mariners on a Lee-shore more earnestly long for the dawning Light than we did now. At Length the Day appeared, but with such dark black Clouds near the Horizon that the first Glimpse of Dawn appeared 30 or 40 Degrees high, which was dreadful enough, for it is a common Saying among Seamen, and true (as I have experienced it), that a high Dawn will have high Winds and a low Dawn small Winds.

We continued our Course still East before Wind and Sea, till about Eight o'clock in the Morning of this 19th Day. Then one of our Malayan Friends cried out Pulo Way. Mr Hall and Ambrose and I thought the Fellow had said Pull away, an Expression usual among English Seamen when they are rowing. And we wondered what he meant by it, till we saw him point to his Consorts and we, looking that way, saw Land appearing like an Island, and all our Malayans said it was an Island at the N.W. end of Sumatra called Way, for Pulo Way means the Island Way. We were dropping with wet, cold and hungry, and were all overjoyed at the Sight of Land, and presently marked its bearing. It bore South and the Wind was still at West, a strong

Gale, but the Sea was not running as high as in the Night. Therefore we trimmed our small Sail no bigger than an Apron and steered with it.

About Noon we saw more land beneath the supposed Pulo Way and, steering towards it, we saw before Night all the Coast of Sumatra, and found the Errors of our Achinese. For the high Land that we first saw, which had then appeared like an Island, was not Pulo Way but a great high Mountain on the Island Sumatra, called by the English Golden Mountain. Then we stuck to our Oars again, though all of us quite tired with our former Fatigues and Hardships.

The next Morning being the 20th Day, we plainly saw all the low Land, and judged ourselves not above eight Leagues off. At Five o'clock in the Afternoon we ran to the Mouth of a River on the Island Sumatra, called Passange Jonca. It is 34 Leagues to the Eastward of Achin and six Leagues to the West of Diamond Point, which makes three Angles of a Rhombus, and is low Land.

Our Malayans were very well acquainted here, and carried us to a small Fishing Village within a Mile of the River's Mouth, also called by the Name of the River Passange Jonca. The Hardships of this Voyage, with the scorching Heat of the Sun at our first setting out, and the cold Rain, and our continuing wet for the last two Days, cast us all into Fevers, so that now we were not able to help each other, nor even so much as get our Canoe up to the Village. But our Malayans got some of the Townsmen to bring her up.

The News of our Arrival being noised abroad, one of the Oramkis came in the Night to see us. We then lay in a small Hut at the end of the Town and, it being late this Lord only viewed us. He spoke with our Malayans and then went away again, but returned to us again the next Day and provided a large House for us to live in till we had recovered from our Sickness, ordering the Townspeople to let us want for nothing. The Achinese Malayans that had come with us told them all the Circumstances of our Voyage: how they were taken by our Ship, and where and how we who had come with them were Prisoners aboard the Ship, and had been set ashore together at Nicobar, as they were. It was probably for this reason that the Gentlemen of Sumatra were thus extraordinarily kind to us, providing everything that we had need of, and forcing us to accept Presents from them that we did not know what to do with, such as young Buffaloes, Goats, &c. These we turned loose at Night, after the Gentlemen that gave them to us had gone, for we were prompted by our Achinese Consorts to accept them, for fear of disobliging by our Refusal. But the Coconuts, Plantains, Fowls, Eggs, Fish and Rice we kept for our use. The Malayans that accompanied us from Nicobar separated themselves from us now, living at one end of the House by themselves. For they were Mahometans, as all those of the Kingdom of Achin are, and though during our Passage by Sea together, we made them be contented to drink their Water out of the same Coco-shell as us, yet being now no longer under that Necessity, they again took up their accustomed Nicety and Reservedness. They all lay sick, and as their Sickness increased, one of them threatened us that if any of them died the rest would kill us for having brought them this Voyage. Yet I question whether they would have attempted it, or the Country People have suffered it. We made a shift to dress our own Food, for none of these People, though they were very kind in giving us anything that we wanted, would come near us to assist us in dressing our Victuals. Nay, they would not touch anything that we used. We all had Fevers and therefore took turns to dress the Victuals, according to the Strength we had to do it, or Stomachs to eat it. I found my Fever increasing, and my Head so distempered that I could scarce stand. Therefore I whetted and sharpened my Penknife in order to let my Blood, but I could not, for my Knife was too blunt.

We stayed here ten or twelve Days in hopes to recover our Health, but finding no Amendment, we desired to go to Achin. We were, however, delayed by the Natives, who had a desire to keep Mr Hall and myself to sail in their Vessels to Malacca, Cudda or other Places where they Trade. Finding us more desirous to be with our Countrymen in our Factory at Achin, however, they provided a large Proa to carry us there, as we were unable to manage our own Canoe. Besides, before this, three of our Malayan Comrades had gone very sick into the Country, and only one of them and the Portuguese remained with us to accompany us to Achin, and they were both as sick as we.

It was the Beginning of June 1686 when we left Passange Jonca. We had four Men to row, one to steer and a Gentleman of the Country who came purposely to give Information of our Arrival to the Government. We were but three Days and Nights in our Passage, having Sea Breezes by Day and Land-Winds by Night, and very fair Weather.

When we arrived at Achin, I was carried before the Shebandar. One Mr Dennis Driscal, an Irishman, and a Resident there in the Factory which our East India Company then had there, was Interpreter. Being weak, I was suffered to stand in the Shebandar's Presence. For it is their custom to make Men sit on the Floor as they do, cross-legged like Tailors. But I had not strength then to pluck up my Heels in that manner. The Shebandar asked me several questions, especially how we dared adventure to come in a Canoe from the Nicobar Islands to Sumatra. I told him that I had been accustomed to Hardships and Hazards, and therefore I had undertaken it with much Freedom. He also enquired concerning our Ship, where she had come from, &c. I told him, from the South Seas; that she had ranged about the Philippine Islands, and had now gone towards Arabia and the Red Sea. The Malayans and the Portuguese were also examined, and confirmed what I declared, and in less than half an Hour I was dismissed with Mr Driscal, who then lived in the

English East India Company's Factory. He provided a Room for us to lie in, and some Victuals.

Three Days after our Arrival here, our Portuguese Man died of a Fever. I do not know what became of our Malayans. Ambrose lived not long after, and Mr Hall was also so weak that I did not think he would recover. I was the best, but still very sick from the Fever, and little likely to live. Therefore Mr Driscal and some other Englishmen persuaded me to take some purging Physic from a Malayan Doctor. I took their Advice, being willing to get Ease. But after three Doses, each a large Calabash of nasty stuff, finding no Amendment I thought to desist from more Physic, but was persuaded to take one Dose more, which I did, and it wrought so violently that I thought it would have ended my Days. I struggled till I had been about twenty or thirty times at Stool. But it worked so quick with me, and with little Intermission, and my Strength was almost spent. I even threw myself down once and for all, and had more than sixty Stools in all before it left off working. I thought my Malayan Doctor whom they had so much commended would have killed me outright. I continued extraordinarily weak for some Days after his drenching me thus. But my Fever left me for over a Week, after which it returned upon me again for a Twelve Month, and a Flux with it.

However when I was a little recovered from the Effects of my Drench, I made a shift to go abroad. And having been kindly invited to Captain Bowrey's House there, my first Visit was to him, who had a Ship in the Road but lived ashore. This Gentleman was extraordinarily kind to us all, particularly to me, and importuned me to go as his Boatswain to Persia where he was bound, with a Design to sell his Ship there. From there he intended to pass with the Caravan to Aleppo, and so home for England. His Business required him to stay some time longer at Achin, I judge, to sell some Commodities that he had not yet disposed of. Yet he chose rather to leave the Disposal of them to some Merchant there and make a short Trip to the Nicobar Islands in the meantime, and on his return to take in his Effects and so proceed towards Persia. This was a sudden Resolution of Captain Bowrey's, presently after the Arrival of a small Frigate from Siam with an Ambassador from the King of Siam to the Queen of Achin. The Ambassador was a Frenchman by Nation. The Vessel that he came in was small, yet very well manned, and fitted for a Fight. Therefore it was generally supposed here that Captain Bowrey was afraid to lie in Achin Road, because the Siamers were now at War with the English, and he was not able to defend his Ship if he should be attacked by them.

But whatever made him think of going to the Nicobar Islands, he provided to sail, and took me, Mr Hall and Ambrose with him, though all of us so sick and weak that we could do him no service. It was some time about the Beginning of June when we sailed out of Achin Road. But we met with the Winds at N.W. and turbulent Weather, which forced us back again in two

Days' time. Yet he gave us each 12 Mess apiece, a Gold Coin which is about the Value of 15d. English. So he gave over that Design, and when some English Ships came into Achin Road, he was not afraid of the Siamers who lay there.

After this he again invited me to his House at Achin, and always treated me with Wine and good Cheer, still importuning me to go with him to Persia. But being very weak and fearing the westerly Winds would create a great deal of trouble, I did not give him a positive Answer, especially because I thought I might get a better Voyage in the English Ships newly arrived, or some others now expected here. It was this Captain Bowrey who had sent the Letter from Borneo directed to the Chief of the English Factory at Mindanao.

A short time after this, Captain Weldon arrived here from Fort St George, in a Ship called the *Curtana* bound to Tonquin. This being a more agreeable Voyage than to Persia at this time of the Year. Besides that, the Ship was better accommodated especially with a Surgeon, and still being sick, I therefore chose to serve Captain Weldon rather than Captain Bowrey. But to go on with a particular Account of that Expedition would be to carry my Reader back again, whom having brought thus far towards England in my Circumnavigation of the Globe, I shall not weary him with new Rambles nor so much swell this Volume as I must, to describe the Tour I made in those remote Parts of the East Indies, from and to Sumatra. In short,

it may suffice that I set out to Tonquin with Captain
Weldon about July 1688, and returned to Achin in the
April following. I stayed here till the latter end of
September 1689 and making a short Voyage to Mal-
acca, returning there again about Christmas. Soon after
that, I went to Fort St George, and staying there about
five Months, I returned once more to Sumatra, not to
Achin but to Bencouli, an English Factory on the West
Coast, where I was Gunner about five Months more.

[. . .]

The Painted Prince

The other Passage I shall speak of, that occurred during this Interval of the Tour I made from Achin, is with Relation to the painted Prince, whom I brought with me into England, and who died at Oxford. For while I was at Fort St George, about April 1690, there arrived a Ship called the *Mindanao Merchant*, laden with Clove-bark from Mindanao. Three of Captain Swan's Men, who had remained there when we left, came in her. From these I had the Account of Captain Swan's Death as related before. There was also one Mr Moody who was Supercargo of the Ship. This Gentleman had bought at Mindanao the painted Prince Jeoly, and his Mother, and had brought them to Fort St George, where they were much admired by all who saw them. Some time after this Mr Moody, who spoke the Malayan Language very well and was a Person very capable of managing the Company's Affairs, was ordered by the Governor of Fort St George to prepare to go to Indrapore, an English Factory on the West Coast of Sumatra, in order to succeed Mr Gibbons, who was the chief of that Place.

By this time I was very intimately acquainted with Mr Moody, and was importuned by him to go with him and to be Gunner of the Fort there. I told him I had always had a great desire to go to the Bay of Bengal, and that I now had an offer to go there with Captain Metcalf, who wanted a Mate, and had already spoken to me. Mr Moody, to encourage me to go with him, told me that if I would go with him to Indrapore, he would buy a small Vessel there and send me to the Island Meangis, Commander of her, and that I should carry Prince Jeoly and his Mother with me (that being their Country), by which means I might gain a Commerce with his People for Cloves.

This was a design that I liked very well, and therefore I consented to go there. It was some time in July 1690 when we went from Fort St George, in a small Ship called the *Diamond*, Capt. Howel Commander. We were about fifty or sixty Passengers in all, some ordered to be left at Indrapore, and some at Bencouli. Five or six of us were Officers, the rest Soldiers to the Company. We met nothing in our Voyage that deserves notice till we came abreast of Indrapore. And then the Wind came at N.W., and blew so hard that we could not get in, but were forced to bear away to Bencouli, another English Factory on the same Coast, lying fifty or sixty Leagues to the southward of Indrapore.

Upon our arrival at Bencouli we saluted the Fort, and were welcomed by them. The same Day we came to an Anchor, and Captain Howel, Mr Moody and the other Merchants went ashore, and were all kindly received by the Governor of the Fort. It was two Days before I went ashore, and then I was importuned by the Governor to stay there to be Gunner of this Fort, because the Gunner was lately dead. And this being a place of greater Import than Indrapore, I should do the Company more Service here than there. I told the Governor that, if he would augment my Salary, which by Agreement with the Governor of Fort St George I was to have had at Indrapore, I was willing to serve him, provided Mr Moody would consent to it. As to my Salary, he told me I should have 24 Dollars per Month, which was as much as he gave to the old Gunner.

Mr Moody gave no Answer till a Week after, and then, being ready to be gone to Indrapore, he told me I might use my own Liberty, either to stay here, or go with him to Indrapore. He added, that if I went with him, he was not certain as yet to perform his Promise in getting a Vessel for me to go to Meangis, with Jeoly and his Mother. But he would be so fair to me, because I had left Maderas on his Account, that he would give me half the share of the two painted People, and leave them in my Possession, and at my Disposal. I accepted the Offer, and Writings were immediately drawn between us.

Thus it was that I came to have this painted Prince, whose Name was Jeoly, and his Mother. They were born on a small Island called Meangis [...] I saw the Island twice, and two more close by it. Each of the three seemed to be about four or five Leagues round, and of a good height. Jeoly himself told me that they all three abounded with Gold, Cloves and Nutmegs. For I showed him some of each sort several times, and he told me in the Malayan Language, which he spoke indifferent well, *Meangis Hadda Madochala se Bullawan*, that is, there is abundance of Gold at Meangis. *Bullawan*, I have observed to be the common Word for Gold at Mindanao, but I do not know whether it is the proper Malayan Word, for I found much difference between the Malayan Language as it was spoken at Mindanao, and the Language on the Coast of Malacca and Achin. When I showed him the Spice, he would not only tell me that there was *Madochala*, that is abundance; but to make it appear plainer, he would also show me the Hair on his Head, a frequent thing among the Indians that I have met with, when they want to express more than they can number. He also told me that his Father was Raja of the Island where they lived, that there were not above Thirty Men on the Island, and about one Hundred Women. He himself had five Wives and eight Children, and one of his Wives had painted him.

He was painted all down the Breast, and behind, between his Shoulders; on his Thighs (mostly in front); and in the Form of several broad Rings, or Bracelets, round his Arms and Legs. I cannot liken the Drawings to any Figures of Animals, but they were very curious, full of great Variety of Lines, Flourishes, Chequered Work, &c., keeping a very graceful Proportion, and appearing very artificial, to the point of Wonder,

Piracy, Turtles and Flying Foxes

especially upon and between his Shoulder-blades. By
the Account he gave me of the manner of doing it, I
understood that the Painting was done in the same
manner as the Jerusalem Cross is made on Men's Arms,
by pricking the Skin and rubbing in a Pigment. But
whereas Powder is used in making the Jerusalem Cross,
those at Meangis use the Gum of a Tree, beaten to
Powder, called by the English Dammar, which is used
instead of Pitch in many parts of India. He told me
that most of the Men and Women on the Island were
thus painted, and that they also all had Ear-rings made
of Gold, and Gold Shackles about their Legs and
Arms. Their common Food, from the Produce of the
Land, was Potatoes and Yams. They had plenty of
Cocks and Hens, but no other tame Fowl. He said that
Fish (of which he was a great Lover, as wild Indians
generally are) was very plentiful about the Island, and
that they had Canoes to go fishing in. They often
visited the other two small Islands, whose Inhabitants
spoke the same Language as they did. This was so
unlike Malayan, which he had learnt while he was a
Slave at Mindanao, that when his Mother and he were
talking together in their Meangian Tongue, I could
not understand one Word they said. And, indeed, all
the Indians who spoke Malayan, and who are the trading and politer sort, looked upon these Meangians as
a kind of Barbarian, and upon any occasion of dislike,
would call them *Bobby*, that is, Hogs, which is the
greatest Expression of Contempt that can be, especially
from the Mouth of Malayans, who are generally Mahometans. And yet Malayans everywhere call a Woman

Babby, by a Name not much different; and *Mamma* signifies a Man, though these two last Words properly denote Male and Female. And as *Ejam* signifies a Fowl, so *Ejam Mamma* is a Cock, and *Ejam Babby* is a Hen. But this is by the way.

He also said that the Customs of those other isles, and their manner of living, was like theirs, and that they were the only People with whom they had any Converse. And that once, as he and his Father, Mother and Brother, with two or three Men more, were going to one of these Islands, they were driven by a strong Wind onto the Coast of Mindanao, where they were taken by the Fishermen of that Island, carried ashore, and sold as Slaves, first being stripped of their Gold Ornaments. I did not see any of the Gold that they wore, but there were great Holes in their Ears, by which it was manifest that they had worn some Ornaments in them. Jeoly was sold to one Michael, a Mindanayan, that spoke good Spanish, and commonly waited on Raja Laut, serving him as our Interpreter, where the Raja was at a loss in any word, for Michael understood it better. He often beat and abused his painted Servant to make him work, but all in vain. For neither fair means, threats nor blows, would make him work as he would have him. Yet he was very timorous, and could not endure to see any sort of Weapons, and he often told me that they had no Arms at Meangis, having no Enemies to fight with.

*

I knew this Michael very well while we were at Mindanao. I suppose that Name was given him by the Spaniards, who baptised many of them at the time when they had footing on that Island. But at the departure of the Spaniards, they were Mahometans again as before. Some of our People lay at this Michael's House, whose Wife and Daughter were Pagallies to some of them. I often saw Jeoly at his Master Michael's House, and when I came to have him so long after, he remembered me again. I never saw his Father nor Brother, nor any of the others that were taken with them. But Jeoly came several times aboard our Ship when we lay at Mindanao, and gladly accepted such Victuals as we gave him, for his Master kept him at very short Commons.

Prince Jeoly lived thus a Slave at Mindanao four or five Years, till at last Mr Moody bought him and his Mother for 60 Dollars, carried him to Fort St George, and from there along with me to Bencouli. Mr Moody stayed at Bencouli about three Weeks, and then went back with Captain Howel to Indrapore, leaving Jeoly and his Mother with me. They lived in a House by themselves outside the Fort. I had no Employment for them, but they both employed themselves. She used to make and mend their own Clothes, at which she was not very expert, for they wear no Clothes at Meangis, but only a Cloth about their Waists. And he busied himself in making a Chest, with four Boards and a few Nails that he begged of me. It was but an ill-shaped odd Thing, yet he was as proud of it as if it had been the rarest Piece in the World. After some time they were both taken sick, and though I took as much care of them as if they had been my Brother and Sister, she died. I did what I could to comfort Jeoly, but he took on extremely, inasmuch that I feared him also. Therefore I caused a Grave to be made presently, to hide her out of his sight. I had her shrouded decently in a piece of new Calico, but Jeoly was not so satisfied, for he wrapped all her Clothes about her, and two new pieces of Chintz that Mr Moody gave her, saying that they were his Mother's, and she must have 'em. I would not disoblige him for fear of endangering his Life, and I used all possible means to recover his Health, but I found little Amendment while we stayed here.

In the little printed Relation that was made of him when he was shown for Sight in England, there was a romantic Story of a beautiful Sister of his, a Slave with them at Mindanao, and of the Sultan's falling in Love with her. But these were Stories indeed. They also reported that this Paint was of such Virtue that Serpents and venomous Creatures would flee from him, for which reason, I suppose, they represented so many Serpents scampering about in the printed Picture that was made of him. But I never knew any Paint of such Virtue, and as for Jeoly, I have seen him as much afraid of Snakes, Scorpions or Centipedes, as myself.

[. . .]

Saint Helena Island and Home

The Island Santa Hellena lies in about 16 Degrees South Lat. The Air is commonly serene and clear, except in the Months that yield Rain, yet we had one or two very rainy Days, even while we were here. Here are moist Seasons to plant and sow, and the Weather is temperate enough as to Heat, though so near the Equator, and very healthy.

The Island is small, not more than nine or ten Leagues in length, and stands 3 or 400 Leagues from the main Land. It is bounded against the Sea with steep Rocks, so that there is no landing but at two or three Places. The Land is high and mountainous and seems to be very dry and poor, yet there are fine Valleys, proper for Cultivation. The Mountains appear bare, only in some Places you may see a few low Shrubs, but the Valleys afford some Trees fit for Building, as I was informed.

This Island is said to have been first discovered and settled by the Portuguese, who stocked it with Goats and Hogs. But it being afterwards deserted by them, it lay as a waste, till the Dutch, finding it convenient to relieve their East India Ships, settled it again. But they afterwards relinquished it for a more convenient Place: I mean the Cape of Good Hope. Then the English

East India Company settled their Servants there, and began to fortify it. But being still weak, the Dutch came about here the Year 1671 and re-took it, and kept it in their Possession. This News being reported in England, Captain Monday was sent to re-take it, who by the advice and conduct of a Man that had formerly lived there, landed a Party of armed Men in the Night in a small Cove, unknown to the Dutch then in Garrison, and climbing the Rocks, got up into the Island, and so came in the Morning to the Hills hanging over the Fort, which stands by the Sea in a small Valley. From there, firing into the Fort, they soon made them surrender. There were at this time two or three Dutch East India Ships, either at Anchor or arriving when our Ships were there. These, when they saw that the English were Masters of the Island again, made sail to be gone, but being chased by the English Frigates, two of them became rich Prizes to Capt. Monday and his Men.

The Island has continued ever since in the Hands of the English East India Company, and has been greatly strengthened both with Men and Guns, so that this Day it is secure enough from the Invasion of any Enemy. For the common Landing-Place is a small Bay, like a Half-Moon, scarce 500 Paces wide, between the two Points. Close by the Seaside are good Guns planted at equal distances, lying along from one end of the Bay to the other, besides a small Fort, a little further in from the Sea near the midst of the Bay. All of which makes the Bay so strong that it is impossible to force it. The small Cove where Captain Monday landed his Men, when he took the Island from the Dutch, is scarce fit for a Boat to land at, and yet that is now also fortified.

There is a small English Town within the great Bay, standing in a little Valley, between two high steep Mountains. There may be about twenty or thirty small Houses, whose Walls are built with rough Stones. The inside Furniture is very mean. The Governor has a pretty tolerable few Soldiers to attend him, and to guard the Fort. But the Houses in the Town stand empty, save only when Ships arrive here. For their Owners all have Plantations farther in the Island, where they constantly employ themselves. But when Ships arrive, they all flock to the Town, where they live all the time that the Ships lie here. For then is their Fair or Market, where they buy such Necessaries as they want, and sell off the Product of their Plantations.

Their Plantations afford Potatoes, Yams and some Plantains and Bananas. Their Stock consists chiefly of Hogs, Bullocks, Cocks and Hens, Ducks, Geese, and Turkeys, of which they have great plenty, and sell them at a lower rate to the Sailors, taking in exchange Shirts, Drawers or any light Clothes. Pieces of Calico, Silks or Muslins, Arack, Sugar and Lime-juice are also much esteemed and coveted by them. But now they are in hopes to produce Wine and Brandy in a short time. For they have already begun to plant Vines to that end, there being a few Frenchmen there to manage that

Affair. This I was told, but I saw nothing of it, for it rained so hard when I was ashore that I did not have the opportunity of seeing their Plantations. I was also informed that they get Manatee or Sea-Cows here, which seemed very strange to me. Therefore enquiring more strictly into the matter, I found the Santa Hellena Manatee to be, by their shapes, and manner of lying ashore on the Rocks, those Creatures called Sea-lions. For the Manatee never come ashore, nor are they found near any rocky Shores, as at this Island, there being no feeding for them in such places. Besides, in this Island there is no River for them to drink at, though there is a small Brook runs into the Sea, out of the Valley by the Fort.

We stayed here five or six Days, all of which time the Islanders lived at the Town to entertain the Seamen, who constantly flocked ashore to enjoy themselves among their Country People. Our touching at the Cape had greatly drained the Seamen of their loose Coins, at which these Islanders greatly repined. And some of the poorer sort openly complained against such doings, saying it was fit that the East India Company should be acquainted with it, so that they might hinder their Ships from touching at the Cape. Yet they were extremely kind, in hopes to get what was remaining. They are most of them very poor, but such as could get a little Liquor to sell to the Seamen at this time got what the Seamen could spare, for the Punch-houses were never empty. But had we all come directly here, and not touched at the Cape, even the poorest People among them would have got something by entertaining sick Men. For commonly the Seamen coming home are troubled, more or less, with scorbutic Distempers, and their only hopes are to get refreshment and health at this Island. These hopes seldom or never fail them, if once they get footing here. For the Islands afford abundance of delicate Herbs, with which the Sick are first bathed to supple their Joints, and then the Fruits and Herbs and fresh Food soon afterwards cure them of their scorbutic Humours. So that in a Week's time, Men that have been carried ashore in Hammocks, and those who were wholly unable to go, have soon been able to leap and dance. Doubtless the serenity and wholesomeness of the Air contribute much to the carrying off of these Distempers, for there is constantly a fresh breeze. While we stayed here, many of the Seamen got Sweethearts. One young Man, belonging to the *James and Mary*, was married, and brought his Wife to England with him. Another brought his Sweetheart to England, each being engaged by Bonds to marry at their Arrival in England. And several other Men were Head over Ears in Love with the Santa Hellena Maids, who, though they were born there, yet very earnestly desired to be released from that Prison, having no other way to compass this but by marrying Seamen or Passengers that touch here. The young Women born here, are but one remove from English, being the Daughters of such. They are well shaped, proper and comely, were they in a Dress to set them off.

*

My stay ashore here was but two Days, to get Refreshments for myself and Jeoly, whom I carried ashore with me. And he was very diligent to pick up such things as the Islands afforded, carrying ashore with him a Bag which the People of the Isle filled with Roots for him. They flocked about him, and seemed to admire him much. This was the last place where I had him at my own disposal, for the Mate of the Ship, who had Mr Moody's share in him, left him entirely to my management, I being to bring him to England. But I was no sooner arrived in the Thames than he was sent ashore to be seen by some eminent Persons; and I being in want of Money, was prevailed upon to sell, first part of my share in him, and by degrees, all of it. After this, I heard he was carried about to be shown as a Sight, and that he died of the Small-pox at Oxford.

But to proceed, our Water being filled, and the Ship all stocked with fresh Provision, we sailed from here in Company of the *Princess Ann*, the *James and Mary* and the *Josiah*, July the 2nd, 1691, directing our course towards England, and designing to touch nowhere by the way. We were now in the way of the Trade Winds, which we commonly find at E.S.E., or S.E. by E., or S.E. till we draw near the Line, and sometimes till we are eight or ten degrees to the North of the Line. For this reason, Ships might shape their course so as to keep on the African shore, and pass between Cape Verd and the Cape Verd Islands, for that seems to be the directest course to England. But experience often shows us that the farthest way about is the nearest way home, and so it is here. For by striving to keep near the African Shore, you meet with more uncertain Winds, and are subject to calms. Whereas in keeping the mid-way between Africa and America, or rather nearer the American Continent till you are North of the Line, you have a brisk and constant gale.

This was the way that we took, and in our passage before we got to the Line, we saw three Ships. Making towards them, we found two of them to be Portuguese, bound to Brazil. The third kept on a Wind, so that we could not speak with her, but we found by the Portuguese that it was an English Ship, called the *Dorothy*, Capt. Thwart Commander, bound to the East Indies. After this we still kept Company with our three Consorts till we came near England, and then were separated by bad weather. But before we came within sight of Land, we got together again, all but the *James and Mary*. She got into the Channel before us and went to Plymouth, giving an account there of the rest of us. Thereupon our Men-of-War who lay there came out to join us and, meeting us, brought us off from Plymouth. There, our Consort the *James and Mary* came to us again, and from there, we all sailed in the company of several Men-of-War towards Portsmouth. There our first Convoy left us and went in. But we did not want Convoys, for our Fleets were then repairing to their Winter Harbours to be laid up. So we had the company of several English Ships to the Downs, and also a Squadron of Dutch who sailed up the Channel, but kept off farther from our English Coast, being bound home to Holland. When we came as high as the South Foreland, we left them standing on their Course, keeping on the Back of Goodwin Sands, and we luffed in for the Downs, where we anchored September the 16th, 1691.